The Honor of Women in Islam

By
Professor Yusuf da Costa
University of Cape Town, South Africa

Islamic Supreme Council of America

Published and Distributed by:
Islamic Supreme Council of America (ISCA)
1400 Sixteenth Street NW, #B112, Washington, DC 20036 USA
Tel: (202) 939-3400
Fax: (202) 939-3410
Email: staff@islamicsupremecouncil.org
Web: http://www.islamicsupremecouncil.org

Publishing Office:
17195 Silver Parkway, #201
Fenton, MI 48430 USA
Tel: (888) 278-6624
Fax: (810) 815-0518

Library of Congress Control Number: 2002100156

ISBN: 1-930409-06-0

Please visit http://www.islamicsupremecouncil.org for more titles in Islamic spirituality and traditional scholarship.

O mankind! Reverence your Lord, who created you from a single person, created, of like nature, its mate, and from them twain scattered countless men and women; reverence Allah through whom ye demand your mutual (rights) and the wombs (that bore you): for Allah ever watches over you. (The Holy Quran 4:1)

Table of Contents

About the
Islamic Supreme Council of America

The Islamic Supreme Council of America (ISCA) is a non-profit, non-governmental religious organization that works closely and proactively with non-Muslim individuals and organizations in presenting Islam as a religion of moderation, tolerance, peace and justice.

Islam – America's fastest growing faith – is too often mischaracterized and marginalized. In an effort to foster mutual respect among all cultures and religions, ISCA stresses the common heritage of Islam, Christianity and Judaism through conferences, seminars, publications, media relations and community outreach efforts.

Since its inception, various American policymakers, mainstream academic institutions, government agencies, regional and global media outlets, and interfaith groups have acknowledged ISCA as the foremost expert on traditional Islam. ISCA supports peace wherever it exists, and the precept of "justice for all," condemning all violations of human rights. ISCA openly and actively denounces all types of terrorism, whether intellectual, cultural, political or ideological.

ISCA supports the non-proliferation of nuclear, biological and chemical weapons, and commits to strengthening the values of charity, family, education and public responsibility in American life. Not affiliated with any government, political party or political agenda, ISCA stresses civil duty, active participation in politics, and taking responsibility for shaping the future of America.

ISCA provides practical solutions for Muslims on a broad range of social issues, which are based on contemporary Islamic legal rulings, many of which are put forth by some of the highest-ranking Islamic scholars from around the world, who comprise the organization's advisory board.

ISCA continues to represent traditional Islamic views at the United Nations, UNESCO, the World Conference on Religion and Peace, US Department of State, other branches of American government, and through various levels of domestic and international media.

ISCA experts have recently been featured on NBC's *The Today Show*, *Dateline NBC, MSNBC, Fox News, CNN, CNN International, National Public Radio, ABC Radio, The Savage Nation* with Michael Savage, and in mainstream print media such as *US News and World Report, Newsweek, Talk Magazine, New York Times, Wall Street Journal, Boston Globe, Washington Post, Washington Times, Chicago Tribune, Toronto Star, Detroit Free Press, Los Angeles Times, San Francisco Chronicle, San Jose Mercury News, London Free Press,* and *London Telegraph.*

The timely release of *The Honor of Women in Islam* marks the beginning of ISCA's effort to communicate the traditional values and principles of Islam to the broader community through the publishing industry. It is our hope that this landmark publication will help its readers to better understand the position of respect and honor that women enjoy in the Islamic faith.

For further information, please visit our website at
http://www.islamicsupremecouncil.org

About the Author

Professor Yusuf da Costa is the former Head of the Department of Didactics at the University of Western Cape in South Africa, and former faculty member at the University of Cape Town. Author of many articles on religion, sociology and geography, Dr. da Costa is relied upon as a religious leader throughout the Cape Town Muslim community.

As a member of the advisory committee of the Islamic Supreme Council of America, Professor da Costa is regularly called upon regarding issues pertaining to the practice of traditional Islam in contemporary pluralistic society.

ISCA's advisors are accredited and experienced Islamic scholars, many of whom are authorized to issue fatwas, or legal rulings. When issued by authorized individuals, these rulings preserve the Islamic legal and social systems and help Muslims to address new and controversial issues that continue to arise as modern civilization evolves.

Upon the request of the Islamic Supreme Council of America, Dr. da Costa undertook the writing of *The Honor of Women in Islam* as a mission to elucidate the true respect and love for women that is uniquely inherent in the Islamic faith.

In detailing the rights and roles of Muslim women, Dr. da Costa relies on authentic Islamic source texts, including the Holy Quran and the sayings of Prophet Muhammad (peace be upon him). In addition, the author presents brief case studies of leading female historical figures to demonstrate the real honor and power women have enjoyed in Muslim society, the likes of which was unheard of in the west until the twentieth century.

If we consider Islam in its traditional form, as practiced by the majority of Muslims throughout the world - and not the handful of fundamentalists to whom our attention is often drawn - we too may witness *The Honor of Women in Islam*

Notes

Quotes from the English translation of Holy Quran - the Islamic holy book revealed to Prophet Muhammad - are italicized and noted as (3:124), which connotes 3rd chapter, 124th verse.

"Ahadith", the Holy Traditions which depict the examples of Prophet Muhammad, are also italicized. Both of these textual sources form the basis of Islamic law and thought.

The following symbols are universally recognized by Muslims and have been respectfully included in this work:

The symbol (s) represents "sallAllahu alayhi wa sallam" (Allah's blessings and greetings of peace be upon him), which is customarily recited after reading or pronouncing the holy name of Prophet Muhammad.

The symbol (a) represents "alayhis-salam" (peace be upon him/her), which is customarily recited after reading or pronouncing the holy names of the other prophets, family members of Prophet Muhammad, the pure and virtuous women in Islam, and the angels.

The symbol (r) represents "radiAllahu anh" (may Allah be pleased with him/her), which is customarily recited after reading or pronouncing the holy names of Companions of the Prophet.

Introduction

The coming of Islam in the early part of 7th century C.E. (Christian Era) totally revolutionized the status of women and gender relationships. This does not mean that Divine Messengers prior to Prophet Muhammad (s) brought teachings on the status of women that entrenched their social and spiritual inferiority, nor that the message brought by Prophet Muhammad (s) was in direct conflict with the message brought by other messengers, such as Prophet Jesus (peace be upon him).

The basic teaching of all Divine Revelation has been to grant to all people, irrespective of gender, the highest position of honor in creation. God Almighty says in the Quran:

> *We have honored the offspring of Adam ... and conferred on them special favors, above a great part of Our Creation. (17:70)*

In light of this verse, there is no way that previous revelations could have brought teachings that debased the status of women. The debasement of women during the long course of history has not been the product of Divine Revelation, but of society.

"Man", to a large degree, has been the major instrument in the general degradation of women. It is also "man" who has corrupted or silenced aspects of the teachings of Divine Revelation to justify this degradation.

This ground-breaking study of Muslim women is intended to empower Muslims through enhanced understanding of Islamic teachings that directly impact the female segment of Muslims, and thus impact the home, the community, nation and the world.

This book examines the great status of women in Islam as established in the Quran and Hadith, and seeks to establish a base from which current anti-Islamic and pseudo-Islamic trends can be dissected.

The book also examines teachings that have been corrupted over time, in large part to accommodate cultural and gender-specific traditions that have no Islamic basis.

It is hoped that, even if in a small way, this book will help all readers, Muslim and others, to better understand and appreciate the unique and elevated status God Almighty has given women, and how to apply Islamic guidance and wisdom to matters that concern women and girls.

Professor Yusuf da Costa
University of Cape Town, South Africa

Chapter 1:

The Status of Women in Pre-Islamic Arabia

At the time of the birth of Prophet Muhammad (s) the Arabian Peninsula was almost unknown to the outside world and of very little economic and political significance. Fisher (1966, p. 150) writes about the Peninsula in the following way:

(Arabia) was a land of mystery, doing a little trade with Syria and Egypt and contributing some mercenaries to the Persian and Byzantine armies, but otherwise as remote and inhospitable as the frozen north.... Arabian society was still in the tribal stage.... Nowhere was there a vestige of an Arab state, a regular army, or of a common political ambition. Nor had they found in religion a stabilizing or unifying factor.

It appeared at the time that the harsh tribal life characteristic of Arab society was far removed from the impact of whatever social and cultural developments had taken place in the neighboring territories and countries. This was especially the case of Central Arabia, despite the existence of a large number of towns and villages, and a large inland trade with native goods. (Hell, 1943, p. 12)

Intense tribal rivalry and loyalty to one's tribe gave rise to constant conflict between the Arab tribes, and created a social environment in which there were constant wars, plundering and looting. According to Iqbal (1967, p. 5):

> Attack, counter-attack, loot, plunder, revenge and vendetta were the evils inherent in the very system of Bedouin life. Blood calls for blood and a blood feud may last for forty years, as it sometimes did. The struggle for existence was strenuous and it

was seldom that a Bedouin sat still…and when he could find no enemy to deal with, he found an outlet for his urge for fighting by attacking his own people.

In a social environment characterized primarily by inter-tribal wars and plundering conducted by the male members of the tribe, the status of women was bound to be inferior. Such women were generally treated with little dignity and respect unless, of course, they were members of the upper classes.

Gender Relationships in Pre-Islamic Arabia

The main features of the status of women and gender relationships in pre-Islamic Arabia were as follows.

Status of Upper Class Women

Women of the upper classes or nobility were treated with considerable esteem. They could own property, had a considerable amount of freedom and blood would even be shed to defend their honor.

Rich women belonging to the upper classes enjoyed more freedoms compared to lower class women, such as right to property, indirect participation in the politics of the time, etc. Hadhrat Khadija (r) belonged to the upper class of her tribe and hence enjoyed those privileges that women of her status had. She (had acquired) a large property from her deceased husband and was able to maintain a wealthy business. However, this was not the norm. (Lone, undated, p. 1)

It appears that women of the upper classes had no disability when it came to the owning of property that she might have received as a dower or gift. In addition she could acquire riches by trade and commerce. (Soorma, 1929, p. 55, quoting Abdur Rahim, 1911. *Muhammadan Jurisprudence*, p. 12)

Institution of Marriage

With regard to marriage, even women of the upper classes had to bend their knees to the general social norms that applied to women:

> Among...the Arabs unlimited polygamy prevailed, prior to the promulgation of Islam. A man might marry as many wives as he could maintain, and repudiate them at will. A widow was considered as a sort of integral part of the heritage of her husband. Hence the frequent unions between stepsons and mothers-in-law which, when subsequently forbidden by Islam, were branded by the name of Nikha-ul-Makht (shameful or odious marriages). Even polyandry was practiced by the half-Jewish, half-Sabean tribes of Yemen. (Soorma, 1929, p. 53, quoting Ameer Ali, 1873, Life and Teachings of Mohamed, p. 225)

Before Islam, a woman was not a free agent in contracting marriage. It was the right of the father, brother, cousin, or any other male guardian to give her in marriage, whether she was old or young, widow or virgin, to whomsoever he chose. Her consent was of no moment.

There was even a practice prevalent of marrying women by force. This often happened on the death of a man leaving widows. His son or other heir would immediately cast a sheet of cloth on each of the widows (except his natural mother), and this was a symbol that he had annexed them to himself. If a widow escaped before the sheet was thrown over her, the heirs of the deceased would refuse to pay the dower. This custom is described as the inheriting of a deceased man's widows by his heirs, who in such cases would divide them among themselves like goods....

There was no restriction as to the number of wives an Arab could take. The only limit was that imposed by means, opportunity and inclinations. Unrestricted polygamy that was sanctioned by usage was universally prevalent. This was exclusive of the number of slave girls that a man might possess....

The limits of prohibited relationship within marriage were narrow and defined by close degrees of consanguinity ... but those among them that followed the Magian religion could marry their own daughters and sisters. An Arab was permitted to take as his wife his stepmother, cousin, wife's sisters and could combine in marriage two sisters or a woman and her niece....

Unrestrained as an Arab was in the number of his wives, he was likewise free to release himself from the marital tie. His power in this connection was absolute and he was not required or expected to assign any reason for its exercise, nor was he under the necessity of observing any particular procedure.... It depended on his discretion whether he would dissolve the marriage absolutely and thus set the woman free or not. He might, if he so chose, revoke the divorce and resume marital connection. Sometimes an Arab would pronounce talaq (divorce) ten times and take his wife back, and again divorce her and then take her back, and so on.

The wife in this predicament was entirely at the mercy of the husband, and would not know when she was free. Sometimes he would renounce his wife by means of what was called a suspensory divorce. This procedure did not dissolve the marriage, but it only enabled the husband to refuse to live with his wife, while the latter was not at liberty to marry again....

The wife among the Arabs had no corresponding right to release herself from the marriage bond. (Soorma, 1929, pp. 53-55, quoting Abdur Rahim, 1911. *Muhammadan Jurisprudence,* pp. 9-11)

Women and Sexual Relations

Sexual relations in pre-Islamic society were therefore totally loose, with women being looked upon as chattel, helpless and trampled upon. In addition to "marriages", prostitution and adultery were rampant. The relationship between the sexes took a number of forms, according to Abu Dawud on the authority of A'ishah – *The Book of Marriage (Aspects of Pre-Islamic Marriage,* p. 1):

1. The first was similar to present marriages. A man would give his daughter in marriage after a dowry had been agreed upon.
2. In the second, the husband would send his wife to cohabit with another man in order to conceive.
3. A third kind allowed a woman to cohabit with a number of men. If a child is born, she would choose any one of those men as the father, and he had to accept.
4. The fourth kind was similar to the third, except that a seeress would be used to "tell" whose child it was.

Temporary Marriage

It appears that temporary marriages or "marriages of pleasure" were also in use among the Arabs already in the 4th century C.E. These marriages were contracted for a fixed period on rewarding the woman. The woman had the right to leave the marriage once the agreed upon period had elapsed. (Gibb & Kramers, 1974, p. 418)

In addition to all these, women accompanied men in the tribal wars, and the winners would cohabit freely with such women. Disgrace would, however, accompany the children conceived from such relations. (*Aspects of Pre-Islamic Marriage,* p. 1)

Female Infanticide

The extent of female degradation in pre-Islamic Arabia was also reflected in the practice of female infanticide.

In proportion to his eagerness to have a son, an Arab father regarded the birth of a daughter as a calamity, partly because of the degraded status of women ... and many fathers used to bury their daughters alive as soon as they were born. (Soorma, 1929, p. 55, quoting Abdur Rahim, 1911. *Muhammadan Jurisprudence*, p. 12)

Inheritance

With regard to succession and inheritance, the customary laws of the pagan Arabs were as follows:

> On the death of an Arab, his possessions, such as had not been disposed of, devolved on his male heirs capable of bearing arms, all females and minors being excluded. The heirship was determined by consanguinity, adoption or compact.... The shares of the different heirs were not fixed.... If there were grown-up sons they probably excluded daughters; wives, sisters and mothers did not inherit at all, but the estate was considered liable for the payment of the widow's dower, and among some tribes at least for her maintenance. (Soorma, 1929, p. 56, quoting Abdur Rahim, 1911. *Muhammadan Jurisprudence*, p. 15-16)

Gender Relations

The status of women and gender relations had a number of prominent features in pre-Islamic Arabia. These were, inter alia:

1. The possession of property and other wealth, and membership of the upper class, gave such women certain privileges with regard to the right to property and marriage not enjoyed by the women of the other classes. This meant that the debasement of upper class women was not as harsh as the debasement of other women in the tribe.
2. The widespread practice of polygamy, adultery and prostitution reduced the social integrity of the institutions of marriage and

divorce, and thus the status of women as wives and mothers, and as respected members of the tribal community.

3. This was worsened by social norms that prevented a wife from having access to the property of her late husband, and norms that made her part of the estate of that husband.

4. Practices such as female infanticide were a reflection of the degree of female degradation.

Chapter 2:

The Status of Women in Pre-Islamic Christianity

To reiterate from the course introduction, the basic teaching of all Divine Revelation has been to grant to all people, irrespective of gender, the highest position of honor in creation. God Almighty says in the Quran: *We have honored the offspring of Adam ... and conferred on them special favors, above a great part of Our Creation.* (17:70)

In light of this verse, by their intrinsic qualities previous revelations could not have brought teachings that debased women or prevented their high status. The debasement of women during the long course of history has not been the product of Divine Revelation, but rather of society. "Man", to a large degree, has been the major instrument in the general degradation of women. It is also "man" who has corrupted or silenced aspects of the teachings of Divine Revelation to justify this degradation.

The sentiments expressed in these lines apply especially to the corruption of the teachings of Prophet Jesus (unto whom be peace) on the status of women:

> The religion which claims to be "Christianity" is certainly not the religion taught by the Nazarene. Jesus had the profoundest respect and love for his mother, the Virgin Mary. Naturally, he respected all women, which can best be illustrated by the protection he gave to the woman taken in sin who was being persecuted by the Jews. (Matt. Vii. 1-5) Christ, a model man,

never degraded women... But there is certainly a great deal of truth in the statement that ... those that came later claiming to be savants and saints of the Church did degrade women, and denied her rightful place in the scheme of things. (Soorma, 1929, p. 40)

Jesus Defied Judaic Customs Applied to Women

There is very little doubt that Prophet Jesus (a), giving expression to Divine Revelation, must have encouraged practices through his teachings that honored all women:

> Certainly, the New Testament Gospels, written towards the last quarter of the first century A.D., acknowledge that women were among Jesus' earliest followers. From the beginning, Jewish women disciples, including Mary Magdalene, Joanna, and Susanna, had accompanied Jesus during his ministry and supported him out of their private means... A Jewish woman honored him with the extraordinary hospitality of washing his feet with perfume. Jesus was a frequent visitor at the home of Mary and Martha, and was in the habit of teaching and eating meals with both women and men... (King, undated, pp. 1-2)

Jesus' examples overthrew many centuries of Jewish law and custom. He constantly treated women and men as equals. He violated numerous Old Testament regulations, which specified gender inequality. As the following examples demonstrate, Jesus refused to follow the behavioral rules established by the three Jewish religious groups of the day: the Essenes, Pharisees and Sadducees.

1. **He ignored ritual purity laws.**
   Mark 5:25-34 describes Jesus' cure of a woman who suffered from menstrual bleeding for 12 years. In Judean society of the day, it was a terrible transgression for a man to talk to a woman other than his wife.

2. **He talked to foreign women.**
   John 4:7 and 5:30 describes Jesus' conversation with a woman of
   Samaria. She was doubly ritually unclean since she was both a
   foreigner and a woman.… Jesus also helped a Canaanite woman,
   another foreigner, in Matthew 15:21. He is recorded as curing her
   daughter of demon-possession.
3. **He taught woman students.**
   Jewish tradition at the time was to deny women to be taught. Rabbi
   Eliezer wrote in the 1ˢᵗ century C.E.: "Rather should the words of the
   Torah be burned than entrusted to a woman…. Whoever teaches his
   daughter the Torah is like one who teaches her obscenity." In Luke
   10:38-42, Jesus taught Mary.
4. **He used terminology that treated women as equal to men.**
   Luke 13:16 describes how he…called (a woman) a daughter of
   Abraham, thus implying that she had equal status with the sons of
   Abraham…. Luke 7:35 to 8:50 describes how Jesus…refers to women
   and men (i.e. "all" people) as children of wisdom.
5. **He accepted women in his inner circle.**
   Luke 8:1-3 describes the inner circle of Jesus' followers: twelve male
   disciples and an unspecified number of female supporters.…
   (*The Status of Women in the Gospels*, undated, pp. 1-2)

Post-Ascension Roles

Due to Jesus' widespread, public treatment of women, after the
Ascension women continued to play prominent roles in the early
movement as missionaries, apostles, leaders in house churches, teachers
and leaders in prayer. Women were also prominent as martyrs and
suffered under torture and painful execution because of their beliefs.

Very soon afterwards, all this changed as teachings advocating the
upgrading of the status of women were declared heretical, and all
evidence of women's early leadership roles was erased or suppressed.
This was done by destroying or changing texts, fabricating traditions,

erasing women from the history of the time, or rewriting women's stories. (King, undated, pp. 2-7)

Degradation of Women by the Church

Spurred on by the teachings of the Church, the degradation of women reached an almost all-time low during the Middle Ages. Perhaps during no other age was the subjection of women so intense, her degradation and deprivation of her humanity so rife through prostitution, adultery and rape, and her status as a chattel so widespread.

The Christian theological justification for the degradation of women lies in the "sin of Adam and Eve" with full blame for the transgression being placed against the name of Eve. In light of this, St. Tertullian (1155-1225) wrote, addressing women:

> Do you not know that you are each an Eve? The sentence of God on this sex of yours lives in this age: the guilt must of necessity live too. You are the Devil's gateway. You are the unsealer of the forbidden tree. You are the first deserter of the divine law. You are she who persuaded him whom the Devil was not valiant enough to attack. You destroyed so easily God's image, man. On account of your desert even the Son of God had to die. (*Statements on the Status of Women by Christian Leaders and Commentators*, undated, p. 2)

Later St. Augustine of Hippo (354-430) added to the above: What is the difference whether it is in a wife or a mother, it is still Eve the temptress that we must beware of in any woman ...I fail to see what use woman can be to man, if one excludes the function of bearing children. (*Statements on the Status of Women by Christian Leaders and Commentators*, undated, p. 2)

There is little doubt that the Church and its teachings entrenched and provided the religious justification for the subjection of woman. Will Durant (*The Age of Faith*, 1950, pp. 825-826) writes:

To priests and theologians woman was ..."a necessary evil, a natural temptation, a desirable calamity, a domestic peril, a deadly fascination, a painted ill." She was still the ubiquitous reincarnation of the Eve who had lost Eden for mankind, still the favored instrument of Satan in leading men to hell. St. Thomas Aquinas ...placed her in some ways below the slave (and) ...Man, but not woman, was made in the image of God. (Quoted by Ansari, 1989, vol. 1, pp. 235-236)

Women Held as Non-Human

At the Council of Macon, towards the end of the sixth century a bishop vehemently denied that women were included in the human species. (Westermarck, _Origin and Development of the Moral Ideas_, 1912-1917, p. 663, quoted by Soorma, 1929, p. 40)

What this, of course, provided was the religious validation for loose and depraved sexual relations at all levels of society. A woman was an instrument, not a human being. Durant (_The Age of Faith_, 1950, pp. 825-826) writes:

Cases of incest were numerous. Premarital and extramarital relations were apparently as widespread as at any time between antiquity and the twentieth century ...Rape was common ...William of Malmesbury describes the Norman nobility as "given over to gluttony and lechery", and exchanging concubines with one another less fidelity would blunt the edge of husbandry. Illegitimate children littered Christendom... (Quoted by Ansari, 1989, vol. 1, p. 217)

The Prostitution of Women

In this social environment, of course prostitution would be rife because it represents the ultimate humiliation of women as women. Durant (_The Age of Faith_, 1950, pp. 825-826) writes:

Prostitution adjusted itself to the times. Some women in pilgrimage, according to Bishop Boniface, earned their passage by selling themselves in the towns on their route. Every army was followed with another army, as dangerous as the enemy. 'The Crusaders', reports Alberts of Aix, 'had in their ranks a crowd of women wearing the habit of men; they traveled together without distinction of sex, trusting to the chances of a frightful promiscuity'...

In Rome, according to Bishop Durand II of Mende (1311), there were brothels near the Vatican, and the pope's marshals permitted them for consideration. The Church showed a humane spirit toward prostitutes...A council at Rouen, in the eighth century, invited women who had secretly borne children to deposit them at the door of the church, which would undertake to provide for them; such orphans were brought up as serfs on ecclesiastical properties.

A law of Charlemagne decreed that exposed children should be the slaves of those who rescued and reared them...Penalties for adultery were severe; Saxon law, for example, condemned the unfaithful wife at least to lose her nose and ears, and empowered her husband to kill her. Adultery was common notwithstanding. (Quoted by Ansari, 1989, vol. 1, p. 218)

Civil and Church Laws on the Status of Women

With regard to her legal status, civil law was either equally or more hostile than what the Church had sanctioned. According to Durant (_The Age of Faith_, 1950, p. 826):

Both (civil and canon law) permitted wife beatings ...Civil Law ruled that the word of women could not be admitted in court (and)...marriage gave the husband full authority over the use and usufruct of any property that his wife owned at marriage. (Quoted by Ansari, 1989, vol. 1, p. 236)

Lecky (_History of European Morals_, 1869, vol. ii, p. 339) writes on this matter as follows:

> In addition to the personal restrictions, which grew necessarily out of the Catholic doctrines concerning divorce and the subordination of the weaker sex, we find numerous and stringent enactments, which rendered it impossible for women to succeed to any considerable amount of property, and which almost reduced them to the alternative of marriage or a nunnery.

The complete inferiority of the sex was continually maintained by the law, and that generous public opinion which in Rome had frequently revolted against the injustice done to girls, in depriving them of the greater part of the inheritance of their father, totally disappeared. Wherever the Canon Law has been the basis of legislation, we find laws of succession, sacrificing the interests of daughters and wives... (Soorma, 1929, p. 42)

Chapter 3:

Gender Equality in Islam

Swiftly and effectively, the Divine Revelation swept aside the social debris of feminine degradation and inferiority, and called into question the validity of all those institutions that entrenched this degradation and inferiority. God Almighty says in the Quran:

> O mankind! Reverence your Lord, who created you from a single person, created of like nature its mate, and from them twain scattered countless men and women; reverence God through whom ye demand your mutual (rights) and the wombs (that bore you): for God ever watches over you. (4:1)

> It is He Who created you from a single person, and made a mate of like nature, in order that he might dwell with her (in love). (7:189)

These verses stress the common origin of human beings, of both genders, and of their belonging together "as mates" for each other. There is no suggestion in these verses of the inherent superiority of the one "mate" over the other. The commonality of origins and the similarity of "nature" are indicative of the equality of footing of both genders at (and since) the beginning of creation.

In this way, Islam "cast in granite" for all time, the status of equality of the "mates". In a well-known tradition, Prophet Muhammad (s) said with regard to this: *Women are the twin halves of men.* However, there is more to this than what has been explained.

The Covenant of Monotheism

At the beginning of time, God Almighty gathered together all of the posterity from the "backs" of "the children of Adam" and addressed them: "Am I not your Lord?" They replied: "Yea, we testify to that."

This Covenant of Monotheism involved the essential spiritual personalities of all of humanity in a "world" that had no physical characteristics. At this original level of "existence" there were no divisions of gender, although each "being" addressed must have had within itself its latent gender characteristics. It was later in the material world that differences in gender came to be highlighted for reasons of feminine social subjection.

The Ability to Create

To elaborate further, it is through the feminine gender that the Divine Attribute of "creating" finds one of its major expressions. It is in her womb that the "new human being" is "created" and "shaped", and it is through this womb that the soul is made to enter the material world.

Within the womb also certain of the major decrees associated with the "new human being" is registered. The Divine honor accorded to the feminine gender in the creative process is immense.

Against this background, the dignity of women as human beings was reaffirmed in respect of her spiritual and moral status, and her propriety and personal rights.

The following verses of the Quran further highlight the unique status afforded to women in Islam, in respect to their spirituality, morality, and the specific rights they hold in various roles.

The Spiritual and Moral Status of Women

> *...unto men the benefit of what they earn and unto women the benefit of what they earn. (4: 32)*

Lo! Men who surrender (unto God) and women who surrender, and men who believe and women who believe, and men who obey and women who obey, and men who speak the truth and women who speak the truth, and men who persevere (in righteousness and women who persevere, and men who are humble and women who are humble, and men who give alms and women who give alms, and men who fast and women who fast, and men who guard their modesty and women who guard their modesty, and men who remember God much and women who remember – God has prepared for them forgiveness and a vast reward. (33: 35)

Whoever works righteousness, man or woman, and has faith, verily to him We will give a new life that is good and pure, and We will bestow on such their reward according to the best of their actions. (16:97)

From these verses we learn:

In matters of spiritual grace both man and woman enjoy equal status and are independent of one another. (Ansari, 1989, vol. ii, p. 187)

There is complete equality between the genders with regard to what God Almighty bestows on them as a consequence of righteous deeds. They are rewarded for their actions independent of gender. Thus, with the exception of prophethood, women can reach with men the highest level of spiritual development.

Chapter 4:

Specific Rights of Women in Various Roles

In this chapter we will examine evidence from Quran and Hadith on specific rights of women in their various roles as humans, daughters, sisters, wives and mothers.

Women's Property and Personal Rights

> ...to men is allotted what they earn and to women what they earn. (4:32)

> Unto the men belong a share of that which parents and near kindred leave, and unto the women a share of that which parents and near kindred leave, whether it be little or much – a legal share. (4:7)

It is related on the authority of Abu Shurayh Khuwaylid that the Prophet of God (s) said: O God! I forbid the violation of the rights of the orphan and of the woman. (Al-Nawawi, undated, vol. i, p. 176)

Her Right To Own Property

Islam decreed a right of which women were deprived both before Islam and after it (even as late as the twentieth century), the right of independent ownership. According to Islamic Law, woman's right to her money, real estate, or other properties is fully acknowledged. This right undergoes no change whether she is single or married. She retains her full rights to buy, sell, mortgage or lease any or all her properties. It is nowhere suggested in the Law that a woman is a minor simply because she is a female. It is also noteworthy that such right applies to her properties before marriage as well as to whatever she acquires thereafter.

Her possessions before marriage do not transfer to her husband and she even keeps her maiden name. She has no obligation to spend on her family out of such properties or out of her income after marriage. She is entitled to the "Mahr" which she takes from her husband at the time of marriage. If she is divorced, she may get alimony from her ex-husband. (Badawi, undated, pp. 8-9)

Her Right To Seek Employment

With regard to woman's right to seek employment, it should be stated first that Islam regards her role in society as a mother and a wife as the most sacred and essential one. Neither maids nor baby-sitters can possibly take the mother's place as the educator of upright, complex-free, and carefully reared children. Such a noble and vital role, which largely shapes the future of nations, cannot be regarded as "idleness".

However, there is no decree in Islam which forbids women from seeking employment whenever there is a necessity for it, especially in positions which fit her nature and in which society needs her most. Examples of these professions are nursing, teaching (especially for children), and medicine.

Moreover, there is no restriction on benefiting from woman's exceptional talent in any field. Even for the position of judge, where there may be a tendency to doubt the woman's fitness for the post due to her more emotional nature, we find early Muslim scholars such as Abu Hanifa and Al-Tabari holding there is nothing wrong with it. (Badawi, undated, p. 9)

Her Right To Inherit

With regard to inheritance, the Quran states:

> *God directs you as regards your children's inheritance: to the male a portion equal to that of two females ... (4:11)*

Commenting on this verse, Ansari (1989, vol. ii, p. 191-192) writes:

> This, however, has nothing to do with the inferiority of women. The real reason behind this inequality in shares is that the male has been given the role of breadwinner for the family. As such, a man is entrusted with the financial burden of himself and his wife and children, while the female has not been entrusted with any financial obligations towards anyone, including her husband and children; indeed, not even herself. Thus, receiving half of the male's share remains for her a distinct advantage, rather than a loss.

Her Right to Give Evidence in Law Suits

God Almighty says:

> *... and get two witnesses out of your own men, and if there are not two men, then a man and two women, such as you choose for witnesses, so that if one of them errs, the other can remind her ... (2:282)*

This law is based on the fact that unlike man, whose sphere of activity is mostly outside the home and who, it is expected, gains a rich experience of and acquires a sharp judgment about people, human nature and the world, the natural sphere of activity for the woman is the home, which does not allow her to acquire the same richness of experience and sharpness of judgment regarding the affairs of the world.

Hence, she is not likely to nor should she be expected to hold her own under the severe strain of cross-examination, because of which any shortcoming on her part as a witness to a case is required to be made up through a second woman's evidence. Also bear in mind that while women in the western nations are accustomed to working outside the home, this is not the case throughout the rest of the world.

Her Right To Remarry

Divorced women were granted the right to remarry by the following verse:

> *When you divorce women, and they fulfill the term of their (iddah) do not prevent them from marrying other men if they mutually agree on equitable terms. (2:232)*

The permission for widows to remarry is contained in the following verse:

> *There is no blame on you if you make an offer of marriage (to a widow) or hold it in your hearts. (11:235)*

Her Right To Be Educated

Perhaps the most progressive decree of Islam with regard to women was their right to an education. Removing the shackles of ignorance and placing women under the control of Divine Law and not of backward social norms and customs was a major step in the "liberation" of women. The fact that they were given access to knowledge meant that they also had access to their rights, and they could demand the protection of the Divine Law when these rights were transgressed.

It is recorded by Al-Bayhaqi that the Prophet of God (s) said: *Seeking knowledge is mandatory on all Muslims, male and female.* (Quoted by Badawi, undated, pp. 5-6)

These rights brought about a major revolution in the treatment of women and granted them what rightfully belonged to them of dignity, deference and economic independence. These rights also dramatically impacted future generations of wives and mothers.

The fact that Islam totally altered their subaltern status meant that their self-respect in the different social roles they fulfilled was totally restored. In another sense, Islam gave new meaning to these social roles by reorganizing family relations on the basis of a divinely ordained respect for each other, which totally ruled out all forms of domestic and social abuse of all ages, and at all levels of society.

The Rights of Female Children

The first revolutionary step taken by Islam in terms of guarding the rights of female children was to ban female infanticide and to consider it a crime like any other form of murder.

> When the female (infant) buried alive, is questioned – for what crime she was killed… (81: 8-9)

> When news is brought to one of them of (the birth of) a female (child), his face darkens and he is filled with inward grief! With shame does he hide himself from his people because of the bad news he has had! Shall he retain her on (sufferance) and contempt, or bury her in the dust? Ah! What an evil they decide on. (16:58-59)

Regarding the treatment and status of women, social and religious reform started in the home. It encouraged a deep feeling of love and kindness towards daughters and gave her a special status in the family.

> It is related on the authority of Anas (r) that the Prophet of God (s) said: One, who rears two girls till they reach maturity, will appear on the Day of Judgment attached to me like two fingers of the hand, and he brought his two fingers together. (Muslim) (Quoted by Al-Nawawi, undated, vol. ii, p. 175)

> It is related on the authority of A'ishah (r) who said: "A woman came to me with her two daughters asking something for them. I did not have anything at the time except a single date, which I gave to her. She divided it between her daughters and did not eat it herself. Thereafter she got up and left. When the Prophet of God (s) came, I told him about

this. He said, 'One who is tried with the rearing of daughters and treats them well, will find that they would be a shield for one from the Fire.'" (Bukhari and Muslim) (Quoted by Al-Nawawi, undated, vol. ii, pp. 175-176)

It is recorded by Ibn Hanbal (r) that the Prophet of God (s) said: "Who has a daughter and he does not bury her alive, does not insult her, and does not favor his son over her, God will enter him into Paradise." (Quoted by Badawi, undated, pp. 5-6)

The Female as a Mother

And we have enjoined on man (to be good) to his parents: in travail did his mother bear him, and in two years was his weaning: show gratitude to Me and to Thy parents: to Me is the final goal. (31:14)

Woman as mother commands great respect in Islam. The Noble Quran speaks of the rights of the mother in a number of verses. It enjoins Muslims to show respect to their mothers and serve them well.... (Doi, undated, p. 3)

Abu Hurairah reported that a man came to the Messenger of God (peace be upon him) and asked: "O Messenger of God, who is the person who has the greatest right on me with regards to kindness and attention?" He replied, "Your mother." "Then who?" He replied, "Your mother." "Then who?" He replied, "Your mother." "Then who?" He replied, "Your father."

In another tradition, the Prophet advised a believer not to join the war against Quraysh in defense of Islam, but to look after his mother, saying that his service to his mother would be the cause of his salvation.

Mu'awiyah, the son of Jahimah, reported that Jahimah came to the Prophet (peace be upon him) and said, "Messenger of God! I want to join the fighting (in the path of God) and I have come to seek your advice." He said, "Then remain in your mother's service because Paradise is under her feet."

In a tradition (Quoted by Al-Nawawi, undated, vol. ii, p. 200), the Messenger of God (s) stressed the need to respect the mother even if she is an unbeliever:

> Asma' bint Abu Bakr al-Siddiq (r) said: "My mother came to Madinah from Mecca to see me, while she was an unbeliever, during the time of the Messenger of God (s). I consulted the Messenger of God (s) saying, My mother has come to me desiring something. Should I establish a connection with my mother? He replied, 'Yes, establish a connection with your mother.'"

Chapter 5:

Women and Marriage

The Female as a Wife

God Almighty says in the Quran:

> *They (your wives) are your garment and you are a garment for them. (2:187)*

Doi (undated, pp. 3-4) writes on the wife:

> Just as a garment hides our nakedness, so do husband and wife, by entering into the relationship of marriage, secure each other's chastity. The garment gives comfort to the body; so does the husband find comfort in his wife's company and she in his. The garment is the grace, the beauty, the embellishment of the body, so too are wives to their husbands as their husbands are to them. Islam does not consider woman "an instrument of the Devil", but rather the Quran calls her "muhsana" – a fortress against Satan - because a good woman, by marrying a man, helps him keep the path of rectitude in his life. It is for this reason that marriage was considered by the Prophet Muhammad (s) as a most virtuous act. He said: "When a man marries, he has completed half of his religion."

Prophet Muhammad enjoined matrimony on Muslims by saying:

> *Marriage is part of my way and whoever keeps away from my way is not from me (i.e. is not my follower).*

God Almighty says in the Quran:

> *And among His signs is this: that He has created for you mates from among yourselves, that you may dwell in tranquility with them; and He has put love and mercy between you. Verily in that are signs for those who reflect. (30:21)*

The Prophet Muhammad (peace be upon him) often expressed praise for virtuous and chaste women. He said:

> *The world and all things in the world are precious, but the most precious thing in the world is a virtuous woman.*

He once told the future khalif, `Umar:

> *Shall I not inform you about the best treasure a man can hoard? It is a virtuous wife who pleases him whenever he looks towards her, and who guards herself when he is absent from her.*

On other occasions the Prophet said:

> *The best a man can have is a remembering tongue (about God), a grateful heart and a believing wife who helps him in his faith.*

> *The best thing in the world is a virtuous wife.*

The Prophet wanted to put a stop to all cruelties to women. He preached kindness towards them. He told the Muslims:

1. Fear God in respect of women.
2. The best of you are they who behave best to their wives.
3. A Muslim must not hate his wife, and if he be displeased with one bad quality in her, let him be pleased with one that is good.
4. The more civil and kind a Muslim is to his wife, the more perfect in faith he is.

The Prophet (s) was most emphatic in enjoining upon Muslims to be kind to their women when he delivered his famous khutba on the Mount of Mercy at Arafat in the presence of one hundred and twenty-four thousand of his Companions who had gathered there for the Hajj al-Wada (Farewell Pilgrimage).

In it he ordered those present, and through them all those Muslims who were to come later, to be respectful and kind towards women. He said:

> *Fear God regarding women. Verily you have married them with the trust of God, and made their bodies lawful with the Word of God. You have (rights) over them, and they have (rights) over you in respect of their food and clothing according to your means.*

He exhorted men to marry women of piety and (for) women to be faithful to their husbands and kind to their children. He said:

> *Among my followers the best of men are those who are best to their wives, and the best of women are those who are best to their husbands. To each of such women is set down a reward equivalent to the reward of a thousand martyrs. Among my followers, again, the best of women are those who assist their husbands in their work, and love them dearly for everything, save what is a transgression of God's laws.*

Once Mu'awiyah asked the Prophet (peace be upon him), "What are the rights that a wife has over her husband?" The Prophet replied: Feed her when you take your food, give her clothes to wear when you wear your clothes, refrain from giving her a slap on the face or abusing her, and do not separate from your wife, except within the house.

Once a woman came to the Prophet with a complaint against her husband. He told her: "There is no woman who removes something to replace it in its proper place, with a view to tidying her husband's house, but that God sets it down as a virtue for her. Nor is there a man who walks with his wife hand-in-hand, but that God sets it down as a virtue for him; and if he puts his arm round her shoulder in love, his virtue is increased tenfold."

Her Role In Domestic Affairs

In the matter of administering the affairs of the home, the husband has been placed "a degree" above the wife. God Almighty says:

> ...and men have been placed a degree above them. (2:228)

This verse is explained by the following one:

> Men are the protectors and maintainers of women because God has given the one more (strength) than the other and because they spend of their wealth (to support them). (4:34)

Thus, in the gender relationship at the domestic level, the husband, by virtue of his strength and his role in maintaining his wife, has been given a position "above" her. This has nothing to do with her status as a woman but has to do with her position in the home as a wife. As a woman she might be vastly superior to him intellectually and spiritually, but as a wife she has a right to be protected and supported by him.

Women as Decision Makers

Part of the dignity granted by Islam to women, has been to grant to her the right to participate in decision-making structures, and to be part of the process of mutual consultation in such decisions:

> ...(The believers are those) who conduct their affairs by mutual consultation. (42:38)

In Islam, women have been granted the right to participate in major decision making as a parent, as an educator, in the medical and legal professions, amongst others, and in all the different fields in which she participates. Such women have, as examples, the role of Sayyidatuna A'ishah (r) who taught many of the Companions (r), and the many female teachers of Imam Shafi'i.

Since the advent of Islam, women have taught how to apply decision-making processes in different religious disciplines. These applications require clarity of mind, the rapid reorganization of ideas, and the presentation of complex arguments.

Islam has opened the doors to women to make contributions to the welfare of communities at all levels and to fully participate in building the nation.

Chapter 6:

Hajar, Mother of the Arabs

Abraham Meets Hajar

Our account starts in Iraq at the time of Prophet Ibrahim (a), when his people flung him into a fire because of his rejection of their gods. God Almighty withdrew the attribute of heat from the fire, and Ibrahim was saved:

> We said: O fire! Be thou cool, and a means of safety for Abraham. (21:69)

Ibrahim did not succeed in liberating his people from paganism. On the contrary, they punished him by throwing him into the fire. God rescued him by allowing him to run away to Palestine together with his wife, Sarah (r). From Palestine he moved on to Egypt, which was then ruled by the Hyksos or Amalekite kings. (Haykal, 1976, p. 24)

Sarah was a very beautiful woman and this was reported to the king. The king felt that the presence of such a woman in his palace would raise his position in the sight of his subjects. He summoned Prophet Ibrahim (a) to the palace and questioned him about his relationship with Sarah. Fearing that the king might kill him if he said he was her husband, he said Sarah was his sister. Asked if she was married, he said nothing. Sarah was taken to the palace by the king's staff, where she was clothed in expensive garments and adorned with costly jewels.

But all the glitter and grandeur of the palace could not make her happy. She wept bitterly, would not eat and remained withdrawn. The king tried to soothe her but without success. Whenever he came near her, he experienced a strange feeling; he felt a sense of fear. After that he just could not touch her. Eventually the truth was revealed to him in a dream, that she was a married woman. The following morning the noble king set Sarah free and presented her with a handmaiden named Hajar. Prophet Ibrahim (a) had been saved by Almighty God from degradation, in a country where he was a helpless stranger. (Najaar, 1992, pp. 38-39)[1]

According to Bukhari (Vol. 4, pp.368-370), Abu Hurairah (r) reported on the matter in the following way:

> *(The King) sent for Abraham and asked him about Sarah, saying: "Who is this lady?" Abraham said: "She is my sister (in belief)." Abraham went to Sarah and said: "O Sarah! There are no believers on the surface of the earth except you and I. This man asked me about you and I told him that you are my sister, so do not contradict my statement."*
>
> *The tyrant then called Sarah and when she went to him, he tried to take hold of her with his hand, but his hand became stiff. This baffled him, and he asked Sarah: "Pray to God for me and I shall not harm you." Sarah asked God to cure him, and he was cured. He tried to take hold of her for the second time, but his hand became stiffer than before. This baffled him more, and he again asked Sarah: "Pray to God for me and I shall not harm you." Sarah asked God again and he recovered.*
>
> *He then called one of his guards, and said: "You have not brought me a human being but a devil." The tyrant then gave Hajar to her as a servant. Sarah went back to Abraham but he was praying. He gestured with his hand, and asked: "What happened?" She replied: "God spoilt the evil plot of the infidel, and gave me Hajar for service." Abu Hurairah (r) then addressed his listeners: "That was your mother, O Bani Ma'al-Sama'."*

(Bani Ma'al-Sama' means "the children of the water of the sky" i.e., the descendants of Ismail (a), the son of Hajar. They were so

---

[1] "Hajar" is also spelled "Hagar", and in one case as "Hajirah". The preference in this account is "Hajar" except where "Hagar" is used in quotations.

called because Ismail (a) was nourished with the blessed water of the Zamzam spring. .)

Return to Palestine

Prophet Ibrahim (a) lived in Egypt for a long time, working very hard. As a result, his wealth increased and he became well known. Unfortunately, every successful person invites jealousy. When Prophet Ibrahim (a) detected that people were jealous of him, he packed up his belongings, accompanied by his wife Sarah and servant Hajar, and returned to the Holy Land of Palestine where he found some people who believed in his message. (Najaar, 1992, p. 39)

Ibrahim Marries Hajar

Despite their years of marriage, Sarah had no child. She suggested to her husband that he should marry their servant, Hajar. He accepted her suggestion and married her. According to Ibn Kathir:

> Abraham's sacred law permitted a man to take a secret concubine along with his legal spouse, as Abraham himself did when he secretly married Hagar along with Sarah.... (Tafsir al-Quran al-'Azim, 1970, pp.71-73, quoted by Ayoub, 1992, p. 252)

Very soon Hajar gave birth to a son, Ismail. Later, after Ismail had become a youth, Sarah bore a son who was called Ishaq. Prophet Ibrahim (a) supplicated for this blessing as follows:

> *Praise be to God who has granted unto me in old age Ismail and Ishaq; for truly my Lord is He, the Hearer of Prayer. (14:39)*

Journey to the Valley of Mecca

Ishaq grew up in the company of his brother, Ismail. The father loved both equally, but Sarah was not pleased with this equation of her son with the son of the [servant] girl Hagar. Once, upon seeing Ismail chastising his younger brother, she swore that she would not live with Hagar nor her son. Ibrahim realized that happiness was not possible as long as the two women lived in the same household; hence he took Hagar and her son and traveled south (towards) the valley of Makkah ...that was a midway place of rest for caravans on the road between Yaman and Sham. The caravans came in season, and the place was empty at all or most times of the year. (Haykal, 1976, p. 26)

After traveling for many days, crossing the harsh desert, they stopped at a barren valley (the valley of Makkah), which had no water or vegetation; a wilderness without a human soul ... This then, was the place (that) God had decreed for his wife and baby. They dismounted here. Prophet Ibrahim (a) handed Hajar some dried food, a container of water, a tent and some other items. With a heavy heart he remounted his camel to begin his return journey, alone. Hajar, clinging to the animal, cried: "O Ibrahim, why are you abandoning us in this forsaken valley? If you do not have any feeling for me at least think of your own flesh and blood. Your son will die of hunger and thirst. We will be exposed to wild animals and the elements of nature, without any protection." Prophet Ibrahim (a) ... told her that he was not acting on his own desire but was carrying out God's Command. (Najaar, 1992, p. 40)

> And remember that Abraham was tried by his Lord with certain commands, which he fulfilled. (2:124)

The words of her husband comforted her. She dried her tears and said: "If this is God's Command, then surely He will not abandon us." (Najaar, 1992, p. 40)

Prophet Ibrahim (a) prayed:

> O our Lord! I have made some of my offspring to dwell in a valley without cultivation, by Thy Sacred House; in order, O our Lord, that they may establish regular prayer: so fill the hearts of some among men with love towards them, and feed them with fruits: so that they may give thanks. (14:37)

Hajar's Unparalleled Fortitude

Surrendering to her fate, Hajar sought strength and patience from God Almighty. After a few days, when the food and water had been used up, she and her baby son were gripped by hunger and thirst. The milk from her breasts had dried up and the baby began crying piteously. Hajar's tears also began to flow. With her tears she dabbed the child's lips. Leaving him on the ground, she ran in search of water or some form of food. She climbed a nearby hillock (which later came to be known as Safa), in order to have a better view of the valley. On the other side she saw another hillock (which later came to be known as Marwa). She ran to it and climbed it, but also found nothing and no one. Frantically she ran back to the first hillock, then from one to the other, completing seven runs. (Najaar, 1992, pp. 40-41)

The Miraculous Appearance of the Zamzam Spring

She returned to the child and found him shrieking. "Mercy, O Lord!" she cried. The child's strength was weakening and his breathing was reduced to short, gasping sounds. With an aching heart, the mother looked helplessly on as her only child was about to die. No further sounds came from his parched throat; only the feeble kicking motions of his feet were visible.

Suddenly, she saw crystal clear water bubbling out of the ground where the baby was kicking the earth with his tiny heels. Hajar poured the refreshing water into the child's mouth and watched delightfully as life returned to his tiny body. With tears of joy she thanked God for His never-ending mercy. (Najaar, 1992, p. 41) The life-giving water that gushed forth is the famous Zamzam.

(Hajar) then closed in the spring so that its water might not be lost in the sand. Thereafter the child and his mother lived in Makkah. Arab travelers continued to use the place as a rest stop, and in exchange for services they rendered to the travelers who came with one caravan after another, Hagar and Ismail were sufficiently provided for. Subsequently a number of tribes liked the fountain water of Zamzam sufficiently to settle there. (Haykal, 1976, p. 27)

The Settlement of Mecca

The first tribe to settle there was the Jurhum tribe traveling from Yemen. They noticed the birds flocking towards this spot, and sent out a scout who reported the presence of water. They directed their caravan towards the water. Hajar was overcome with joy to see people in this forsaken land. She saw their arrival as a sign of God's guardianship over her and her son. God had indeed filled the hearts of some among men with love towards them where she and her son had been abandoned. Ibrahim's prayer for his family had been answered. (Najaar, 1992, p. 41)

The tribe said to her: "If you will share with us the water of this spring, we will share with you the milk of the herds." (Hughes, undated, p. 154, quoting *Tafsir al-Baydhawi*, p. 424)

Hajar welcomed them heartily as her honored guests. They sent for their families and many of them made Mecca their permanent home. Ismail grew into a fine young man, and married a girl from the Jurhum tribe who bore him twelve sons.

These (sons) were the ancestors of the twelve tribes of Arabized or Northern Arabs. On their mother's side they were related through Jurhum to the Arabized Arabs, the sons of Ta'rub ibn Qahtan. They were also related to Egypt through their grandmother on their father's side, Hagar, which was a close relation indeed. Through their grandfather, Ibrahim, they were related to Iraq and Palestine.... (Haykal, 1976, pp. 27-28)

Hajar as a Role Model

There are a number of important lessons we learn from this account of Sayyidatuna Hajar (a), highlighted by the great honor God has paid her.

1. **The First Settler of Mecca**

   She is associated with the first settlement at Mecca. She and her son Ismail were most probably the first persons to establish residence there. At the time, the Ka`ba had not yet been built and the valley of Mecca was only used as a throughway for caravans. It would, therefore, not be historically wrong to refer to her and her son as the first inhabitants of the holiest place in the cosmos.

2. **Honored in Hajj and `Umra**

   Her running between Safa and Marwa, as the hills were later called, became an integral part of the Hajj and `Umra known as "the Sai", permanently established in Islam as a form of worship. What was originally a search for water became elevated to a means of approach to God Almighty.

   Hajar's passion in the search to save their lives transformed her running into a race towards God Almighty. All those who perform the Hajj and `Umra have now to imitate her in that running. Thus, the action of an Egyptian servant was later confirmed by the Prophetic practice to be an essential part of one of the obligations of Islam.

3. **The Miracle of Zamzam**

   Her and her son's presence caused the spring of Zamzam to start flowing. This spring is one of the major contributory factors for the habitation of the area that became Mecca, and the launching of the large number of historical events associated with the city.

4. **Mother of the Muslim Nation**

   Sayyidatuna Hajar, through her son and his children, was the beginning of the Arab nation that eventually produced the Final Messenger, Muhammad (s).

5. **Sublime Example of Submission**

Perhaps the major lesson we learn from her was the extent to which she submitted her will, without any reservations, to the Will of God Almighty. She did not object to being left in the valley of Mecca by Prophet Ibrahim (a) because it was what God had willed. Totally depending on God Almighty for their protection and survival, she was satisfied when her husband left her and her son in the desolate valley. Her strength and spirit of determination reflected a level of near incomparable reliance on God and spiritual proximity to Him.

Chapter 7:

Mary Mother of Jesus,
One of the Greatest Spiritual Figures
of All Time

Sayyidatuna Maryam (r)

God Almighty honored Maryam, Mother of Jesus (a), with the miracle of the virgin birth. The Quran narrates several accounts of her, and even a chapter of the Quran is named for her.

> *God chose Adam and Noah, the house of Abraham and the house of 'Imran above all things. They all are of one progeny, one following the other. God is All-Hearing, All-Knowing. Remember when the wife of 'Imran said: "My Lord, I have vowed to you that which is in my womb, a pure dedication. Accept it from me! You are the All-Hearing, the All-Knowing." When she gave birth to her, she said: "Lord, I have delivered her a female – yet God knows best what she delivered – and the male is not as the female. I have called her Mary, and I seek refuge in You for her and her progeny from the accursed Satan."*

> *Thus her Lord received her with gracious acceptance and nurtured her into gracious maturity. He placed her in Zachariah's custody. Whenever Zachariah went into her prayer chamber, he found her well provisioned. He said: "Mary, whence comes this to you?" "From God," she said, "God surely provides whomsoever He wills without reckoning." (3:33-37)*

There is considerable agreement that the 'Imran mentioned in the verses is 'Imran, father of Mary, the mother of Prophet Isa (a). (Ayoub, 1992, vol. ii, pp.85-93). Imran's genealogy goes back to Prophet Dawud (a).

Imran's wife was called Hannah, daughter of Fadugh, son of Qabil. (Tabari, *Jami' al-Bayan 'an Ta'wil Ay al-Quran,* 1961-1969, vol. vi, pp. 328-329, quoted by Ayoub, 1992, vol. ii, p. 93)

Zechariah and 'Imran married two sisters. The mother of Yahya (John the Baptist) was with Zechariah, and the mother of Mary was with 'Imran. 'Imran, however, died while his wife was pregnant with Mary. It has come to us that the wife of 'Imran was barren until she reached old age. 'Imran and his family were people of high status with God.

While she sat one day in the shade of a tree, Hannah saw a bird feeding its young. Thus she yearned for offspring, and prayed God to grant her a child. God answered her prayers, and she conceived Mary. Shortly thereafter 'Imran died. When his wife ascertained her pregnancy, she vowed to dedicate the child in her womb to the service of God. The custom was that such a child would worship God and serve the Temple in total isolation from all affairs.

Hannah gave birth to a baby girl. She again turned to God, and spoke the famous words: "Lord, I have delivered her a female – yet God knows best what she delivered – and the male is not as the female. I have called her Mary...." (Quoted by Ayoub, 1992, vol. ii, p.93)

Interpretation of Hannah's Prayer

These words of Hannah have been interpreted in various ways, according to Ayoub, 1992, pp. 94-99:

> The male is stronger than the female and more able to endure the hardship of the service in the Temple than the female. Moreover, the female is unable in certain circumstances to enter the sacred precincts to perform her duties in the Temple because of impurities associated with menstruation. (Tabari, 1961-1969, vol. vi, p. 334)

These words of Hannah reflect her status as a mystic of the first order. It is as if she had said: "My desire was for a male, but this female is God's gift to me. Thus the male whom I desired is not as the female whom I have offered to God." This indicated her strong belief that what God does with His servant is far better than what the servant desires for him/herself. (Razi, undated. *Al-Tafsir al-Kabir*, vol. viii, pp. 26-29)

Hannah spoke out of sorrow and disappointment for not getting a male child. God's assurance to her was because He knew best the child she had given birth to and the impact she and her child would have on the course of human history. (Zamakhshari, *Al-Kashshaf 'an Haqa'iq al-Tanzil wa 'Uyun al-Aqawil fi Wujuh al-Ta'wil,* 1966, vol. I, pp. 355-357)

She named the child Mary because in her language it meant *al-abidah*, the worshipping maidservant. By this she hoped that God would protect her child from error so that her actions might concur with her name. (Zamakhshari, *Al-Kashshaf 'an Haqa'iq al-Tanzil wa 'Uyun al-Aqawil fi Wujuh al-Ta'wil,* 1966, vol. I, pp. 355-357)

Seeking Refuge in God

Hannah concluded her supplication with the words:

> ... *I seek refuge in You for her and her progeny from the accursed Satan.*

It is related on the authority of Abu Hurairah that the Messenger of God (s) said: Every newborn of the children of Adam must endure the stab of Satan's (finger), which causes the child to cry out, except Mary daughter of 'Imran and her son. This is because when her mother gave birth to her, she said: "I seek refuge in You for her and her progeny from the accursed Satan." A curtain was drawn between them and Satan stabbed the curtain instead. (Ayoub, 1992, p. 94)

A Daughter Serving the Temple

Hannah had a big problem about her promise to God: females were not accepted into the temple. She was very worried. Her sister's husband, Zechariah, comforted her, saying that God knew best what she had delivered, and appreciated fully what she had offered in His service. So she wrapped the baby in a shawl and handed it over to the temple elders.

As it was a baby girl, the question of her guardianship posed a problem for the elders. Because this was a child of their late and beloved leader, 'Imran, everyone was eager to take care of her. Zechariah said to the elders: "I am the husband of her maternal aunt, and her nearest relation in the temple. I will therefore be more mindful of her than all of you." (Najaar, 1992, p. 134)

They decided to cast lots to settle the dispute. God Almighty says about this:

> *For you were not with them when they were casting their quills who among them should have custody of Mary, nor were you with them when they were disputing. (3:44)*

According to Tabari (1961-1969, vol. vi, pp. 345-351), quoted by Ayoub, 1992, vol. ii, p.99:

> It has come down to us that when Zechariah and his opponents disputed concerning Mary, as to who should have charge of her, they cast lots with arrows in to River Jordan. Some of the men of learning have related that Zechariah's arrow stood firm, so that it was not washed away by the water, while the arrows of all the others were washed away. At this sign they all surrendered to the will of God and made Zechariah the guardian:

> ...when she grew up he built a prayer chamber for her which could only be reached by a ladder. No one went to see her except Zechariah until she reached maturity. During the days of her menstruation, Zechariah would take Mary to his home to stay with her aunt until she was clean. Then he would take her back to her chamber. (Qurtubi, 1967. Al-Jami' li-Ahkam al-Quran, vol. iv, pp. 69-71, quoted by Ayoub, 1992, vol. ii, p. 102)

Miracles Associated with Maryam

As she grew up, she spent her time in devotion to God. Zechariah visited her daily to see to her needs. This continued for many years, and during that time she grew in "wisdom, chastity and obedience", and was blessed with karamat (miracles). (Ayoub, 1992, vol. ii, p. 102).

Some time later the Children of Israel suffered a famine. Thus Zechariah went before them and said: "O Children of Israel, by God I can no longer support the daughter of 'Imran." They thus cast lots, and the man chosen was a carpenter called Jurayj. Mary noticed his anxiety and said: "O Jurayj, think well of God, for he shall provide for us!" God multiplied the provisions that Jurayj took to Mary in her prayer chamber in the Temple. Thus, when Zechariah went to see her, he asked, "Mary, whence comes this to you?" "It is from God," she answered. (Tabari, 1961-1969, vol. vi, pp. 353-357, quoted by Ayoub, 1992, vol. ii, p. 100)

There is also another interpretation of the provisions supplied to Mary by God Almighty (Nisaburi, 1962-1970, *Ghara'ib al-Quran wa Ragha'ib al-Furqan,* vol. iii, p. 186, quoted by Ayoub, 1992, vol. ii, p. 103):

These were provisions of the revelations with which God nourishes His servants, those who spend their nights with Him and not with any of his creatures. This is in accordance with the Prophet's saying: *"I spend the night with my Lord, and He provides me with nourishment of food and drink."*

Zechariah understood by this that God had raised Mary's status above other women. Thereafter, he spent more time with her, teaching and guiding her. Mary grew up to be a devotee of God, glorifying Him day and night. (Najaar, 1992, p. 134)

The Prayer of Zechariah

While Mary, in almost permanent seclusion, was making these massive spiritual strides, Zechariah, inspired by Mary, was generating his own spiritual experience of a very high order. It must have been extraordinary – both historically and religiously - for two such spiritual luminaries to be virtually in daily contact with each other.

> *Thereupon Zechariah prayed his Lord saying: "My Lord, grant me from you an offspring, for surely you are the Hearer of prayers!" Then the angels called to him while he was standing at prayer in the sanctuary: "God gives glad tidings of John, confirming a Word of God, a master, a chaste man and a prophet, one of the righteous." He said: "My Lord, how shall I have a male child when I have reached old age and my wife is barren?"*

> *He answered: "Thus will it be, for God does what He wills." Zechariah said: "Lord, give me a sign!" "Your sign," said He, "shall be that you will not speak to the people for three days except by gestures. Remember your Lord much and give glory in the evenings and early mornings." (3:38-41)*

While this miracle was in the process, Mary came to a stage of truly magnificent spiritual development, a level that established her spiritual uniqueness and dominance generally amongst all women of all time.

> *Remember when the angels said: O Mary, God has surely chosen you above the women of humankind. O Mary, be obedient to your Lord, prostrate yourself and bow down with those who bow down. (3:42-43)*

According to Tabari (1961-1969, vol. vi, pp. 393-398, quoted by Ayoub, 1992, vol. ii, p. 123), God Almighty had chosen Maryam for His obedience and for the special favors He had bestowed on her. Thus He purified her faith from all doubts and impurities. It is for these reasons that He chose her to be above all women "of her time" and made her the most excellent of women. Tabari mentions a number of traditions with regard to this:

> *The Messenger of God (s) said: The best of the women of the people of Paradise are Mary, daughter of 'Imran, and Khadijah, daughter of Khuwaylid. [On the authority of Ali (r).]*

The Messenger of God (s) said: "The best of the women of humankind are Mary, daughter of 'Imran, Asiyah, [daughter of Muzahim and] wife of Pharaoh, Khadijah, daughter of Khuwaylid, and Fatimah, daughter of Muhammad." (On the authority of Qatadah (r).)

The Messenger of God (s) said: "Many among men attained perfection, but the only women who attained perfection were Mary, Asiyah, the wife of Pharaoh, Khadijah, daughter of Khuwaylid, and Fatimah, daughter of Muhammad." (On the authority of Abu Musa al-Ash'ari (r).)

Some scholars, such as Qurtubi, who were of the opinion that Mary was chosen to be above all women "for all time", and that she was a prophetess because she had received revelation from Jibril (a). Whatever the case might be, she had reached the stage of "perfection" in her spiritual development through a process of "purification" that God Almighty had put her through.

Maryam's Sanctified Purity

According to Razi (undated, *Al-Tafsir al-Kabir*, vol. viii, p. 45-46, quoted by Ayoub, 1992, vol. ii, p. 123), Sayyidatuna Maryam was purified from:

1. Rejection of faith and disobedience
2. Being touched sexually
3. Menstruation
4. Bad actions and habits, and
5. Suspicion and accusations

The Blessed Conception and Birth

And then the next great miracle, in which Mary is the central figure, commenced. While Mary was praying in the temple, a number of angels appeared before her:

When the angels said: "O Mary, God gives you glad tidings of a Word from Him whose name is the Messiah, Jesus, son of Mary, highly honored in this world and the next, and one of those brought near (to God). He shall speak to the people in the cradle and in the middle age, and shall be one of the righteous." She said: "My Lord, how shall I have a child when no man has touched me?" He said: "Thus shall it be, for God creates whatever He wills. When He decrees a thing, He but says to it: Be! And it is." (3:45-47)

The visit by the angels caused Mary great anxiety. As the months went by her anxiety increased. How could she face the question of giving birth to a child without having a husband? Later, she felt life kicking inside her. With a heavy heart she left the temple and went to Nazareth, the city in which she was born. She settled in a simple farmhouse to avoid the public. But fear and anxiety did not leave her. She was from a noble and pious family, whose branches forked out in the distant past. Her father was not an evil man nor was her mother an impure woman, but how could she prevent tongues from wagging about her honor? After some months, she could not bear the mental strain any longer, and burdened with a loaded stomach she left Nazareth, not knowing where to go, but anywhere, to be away from this depressed atmosphere.... (Najaar, 1992, p. 135)

When she reached Bethlehem to the south of Jerusalem, she was overtaken by the pains of childbirth. She sat down against a dry palm tree. Here she gave birth to a son. She was hurt that she had brought him into the world without a father. *(Najaar, 1992, p. 134)*, and exclaimed:

> *Ah! Would that I had died before this! Would that I had been a thing forgotten and out of sight! (19:23)*

Here, we see Sayyidatuna Maryam is intensely human. The anguish of having to give birth with no one to attend to her, and the anxiety over the possibility of social rejection and derision for giving birth to a child as an unmarried woman caused her to cry out in anguish. The emotional pain was almost unbearable, and God Almighty assures and calms her:

> *Grieve not! For thy Lord hath provided a rivulet beneath thee; and shake towards thyself the trunk of the palm tree; it will let fall fresh ripe*

dates upon thee. So eat and drink and cool (thine) eye. And if you see any one say, "I have vowed a fast to (God), Most Gracious, and this day will I enter into no talk with any human being." (19:24-26)

As she expected, her arrival in the city with a newborn babe on her arms aroused the disgust of the people:

O Mary! Truly an amazing thing hast thou brought! O sister of Aaron! Thy father was not a man of evil, nor thy mother a woman unchaste. (19:27-28)

The amazement of the people knew no bounds. In any case they were ready to think the worst of her, as she had disappeared from her kin for some time. But now she comes, shamelessly parading a babe in her arms! How she had disgraced the house of Aaron, the fountain of priesthood! We may assume the scene took place in the Temple in Jerusalem, or in Nazareth ...What could Mary do? How could she explain? Would they in their censorious mood, accept her explanation? All that she could do was to point to the child ...(Ali, undated, p. 773)

But she pointed to the babe. They said: "How can we talk to one who is a child in the cradle?" He said: "I am indeed a servant of God: He hath given me revelation and made me a prophet; and He hath made me blessed wheresoever I be, and hath enjoined on me prayer and zakah as long as I live. He hath made me kind to my mother, and not overbearing and miserable. So peace is on me the day I was born, the day I die, and the day that I shall be raised up to life (again)." (19:29-33)

Mary reared her son, sent him to school and later when he commenced his work as a Messenger of God, she accompanied him; testifying to the truth of his words. Her historical role slowly fades as that of her son gains prominence. God Almighty speaks about her in the Quran in the following way:

And Mary the daughter of Imran, who guarded her chastity; and we breathed into (her body) of Our Spirit; and she testified to the truth of the Words of her Lord and His revelations, and was one of the devout servants. (66:12)

She had attained the highest possible "spiritual dignity". The fact that the word "qanitin" (devout) is not in the feminine gender indicates that she was functioning spiritually at a level at which gender has no meaning. (Ali, undated, p. 1574)

Maryam's Unparalleled Honor

Maryam Mother of Jesus (a) stands out amongst all people, and not only women, as one of the greatest servants of God. Although not a prophetess (if one accepts that view), she is one of the greatest examples amongst women of spiritual attainment through concentrated personal sacrifice. Almost permanently in seclusion and in the remembrance of God, she was prepared to bring forth into the world the only Messenger of virgin birth. And when she did so, Divine Grace (wilayah) flourished in her and she spiritually surpassed all women and most men.

The unprecedented historical process that commenced with her has still to be fulfilled when her noble son, the second-to-last Messenger Jesus (a) returns to complete certain world-shaping duties.

Chapter 8:

The Early Muslim Women Pioneers

As we have previously acknowledged, with its introduction fifteen centuries ago, Islam faced a system of female degradation entrenched by the Church, State and social tradition. Islam, through its teachings, raised women back onto their feet by giving recognition to their humanity and granting them their dignity and self-respect as women.

This presented one of the world's major revolutions in human thought and practice; a revolution grudgingly admitted to by some, totally denied by others. The fact, however, remains that Islam gave back to women their rights to property, to inherit, to remarry, to an education, to give evidence, to make decisions and to seek employment. And it is Islam that gave recognition to their spiritual and moral status, and to their status as daughters, wives and mothers.

The first women who benefited in a variety of ways from this "major revolution in human thought and practice" were the immediate family members of Prophet Muhammad (s). Along with the women of Madinah, these were the first beneficiaries of a social order that gave recognition to their humanity and granted them their dignity and self-respect as women. Their response to the new social order, and the dignity they brought to their newly gained recognition, rights and status, laid the foundation for the blossoming of intellectuality and spirituality of women in later generations.

The Unique Status of Women in the Time of the Prophet

Al-Ismail (1988, p. 193) explains:

> Each of the women who entered the life of the Messenger, and in consequence into the life and customs of all Muslims, was of well-known and noble lineage. Each of them in her own way was exemplary as an individual, and each had special characteristics or circumstances that made it imperative for Muslims to study her life and emulate it. The women in the life of the Messenger were exceptional women, just as the men who helped him were very great indeed, but besides the overpowering light of the Messenger they seemed no different from the common run of men. It is when each is studied apart and individually that one discovers how truly great these early Muslims were.

How the Prophet's Wives (r) Contributed to the New Social Order

Here we will examine roles of Ummat al-Mumineen, "Mothers of the Faithful" (i.e. The Prophet's Wives, radhiAllahu anhum) who made a tangible contribution to the new social order. While almost all the wives were transmitters of ahadith, not all of them made lasting impacts that have been recorded by historians.

Sawda bint Zam'a ibn Qays ibn Abdu Shams

Prophet Muhammad (s) was married to Sayyidatuna Khadijah (r), his only wife at the time, for a period of twenty-eight years. When she passed away, he married Sawda (r), the widow of Sakran ibn 'Amr ibn Abd Shams. She belonged to the famous Quraysh tribe. Her father was Zam'a ibn Qays. Her mother, Shamus, belonged to the Bani Najjar of Madinah.

Sawda was the wife of one of the early converts of Islam who suffered much harm for the sake of the faith and who had migrated to Abyssinia following the instructions of the Prophet in order to find a measure of safety. Sawda had embraced Islam with her husband and migrated with him. She suffered as he did and bore Makkan oppression as patiently as her husband did. (Haykal, 1976, p. 290)

Her husband died a few days after their return from Abyssinia. In the meantime Sayyidatuna Khadijah had died, and Prophet Muhammad (s) "was very depressed and dejected". When Sawda's waiting period was over, he sent Khawla bint Hakim, the wife of `Uthman ibn Maz'un, to Sawda's father with a proposal of marriage. Her father replied: "No doubt Muhammad (s) is a noble man, but I would like to consult Sawda first." She agreed, and they were married in Ramadan, the tenth year of his prophethood. (Siddiqi, 1982, p. 21) She migrated with him to Madinah.

Sawda's Prominent Achievements

Many of Sayyidatuna Sawda's characteristics stand out very prominently and contributed greatly to the new social dispensation.

1. **She desired to be included among the Mothers of the Believers.**
   It is related from al-Qasim ibn Bazza that the Prophet (s) had sent (a message) to Sawda about divorcing her. When he came to her, she waited on his way by A'ishah's room. When she saw him, she said, "I adjure you by the One who sent down His Book on you and chose you over His creation. Why do you wish to divorce me? Do you have some ill-feeling towards me?" He said, "No." She said, "I adjure you by the like of the first, will you take me back! I am old and have no need of men but I want to be raised up among your wives on the Day of Rising." So the Prophet (s) took her back, and she said, "I have given my day and night to A'ishah, the beloved wife of the Messenger of God (s)." (Ibn Sa'd, 1995, p. 40)

2. **She was implicitly obedient to God and His Prophet (s).**

   The Holy Prophet while addressing his wives on the occasion of the Hajj al-Wada' said, "When I leave, do not go out of the house." Hadrat Sawda acted upon this advice strictly and did not proceed for Hajj after this. She said, "I have performed both Hajj and 'Umra and I shall remain in the house according to the Will of God." (Siddiqi, 1982, p. 23-24)

3. **She participated in the education of Muslims and the spread of Islam.**

   Companions such as Ibn 'Abbas, Ibn Zubayr and Yahya ibn Abd al-Rahman transmitted from her. (Siddiqi, 1982, p. 23)

4. **She was firm in her religious convictions.**

   As noted above, she refused to accept a divorce from the Messenger of God (s) and negotiated agreeable terms for him to keep her as his wife.

5. **She was known for her hospitality and generosity.**

   Once Hadrat 'Umar (God be pleased with him) sent to her a bag. She enquired, "What is in it?" He replied, "Dirhams." She said, "Dirhams are also sent in a bag like dates," and then she distributed all (the dirhams). (Siddiqi, 1982, p. 24)

6. **She was socially independent.**

   Her father sought her consent before marrying her to the Messenger of God (s).

A'ishah bint Abu Bakr al-Siddiq

At about the same time that the Messenger of God (s) married Sawda, he also married A'ishah, daughter of Sayyiduna Abu Bakr al Siddiq and Zaynab (may God be pleased with them all).

A'ishah herself was quite a unique personality destined to play a unique and vital role in the history of Islam. She was exceptionally attractive and graceful, affectionate and of radiant countenance, but her greatest endowments were her quick wits and phenomenal memory. From her father as-Siddiq, she inherited a quiet strength and confidant attitude.

From his learning, she acquired a good knowledge of history, the language, the poetry and lineage of Arabia. Of relatively well-to-do background, she was brought up dignified and charity loving. All these character traits combined to make her a most engaging and intriguing personality. Perhaps no young girl of the Quraysh was more qualified than her to occupy the role of the wife and partner of a Prophet and a statesman. (Bashier, 1990, pp. 148-149)

One of the Greatest Minds in Islam

Sayyidatuna A'ishah stands out as one of the great minds of her time, having accumulated a wealth of Islamic knowledge from her husband during a period of about ten years in his company as his wife.

The tasks of learning the Quran, its interpretation, the Sunnah of the Prophet, and the intricate, complex issues of Islamic Jurisprudence and law, are so exacting that only a person with extraordinary intellectual abilities could have been equal to them. (Bashier, 1990, p. 149)

It is perhaps for this reason that the Messenger of God (s) said about her:

> Take half your religion from this _humayra_ (red-faced lady).

A number of scholars had attested to her intellectual greatness. Imam al-Zuhri stated that she was the most learned of the Muslims, and that the senior and learned Companions used to consult her. Urwah ibn al-Zubayr referred to her as:

> ...the most scholarly person in the sciences of the Quran, poetry, fiqh, medicine, history of the Arabs, their genealogy, and was the most competent in distinguishing between halal and haram. She ranked, with `Abdullah ibn Abbas, `Ali ibn Abi Talib, `Umar ibn al-Khattab and `Abdullah ibn Mas'ud, among the five most learned Muslim Companions of the Prophet *(Bashier, 1990, pp. 149-150).*

According to (Siddiqi, 1982, pp. 35-26):

> She used to issue religious verdicts during the time of Sayyiduna Abu Bakr, `Umar and `Uthman (r). Her review of the writings of some of the Companions has been compiled into a journal by Imam Suyuti.

She narrated about 2,210 Prophetic traditions of which Imam Bukhari mentions 54 and Imam Muslim 68. It is said that one-fourth of the traditions relating to the Shari'ah had been reported on her authority.

She wrote on a variety of matters including, inter alia, the existence of God, knowledge of the Unseen, the innocence of Prophets, the Mi'raj, the order of the revelation of the Quran, Jumu'ah, Qasr Salah, the fast of 'Ashura, and Hajj.

She was famous as an eloquent speaker. Musa ibn Talha (r) said about her, "I have never seen a person more eloquent than A'ishah." It is considered that the only persons who surpassed her in excellence in eloquence were Sayyiduna `Umar and `Ali (r). The speeches she delivered at the Battle of the Jamal have very few parallels in style.

She was foremost in her knowledge of Arab history. She related accounts of the conditions of the pagan Arabs; their rites and rituals, genealogies and their social life. She recorded important events in Islamic history.

Although she was not a poetess, she had memorized large pieces of poetry such as the whole eulogy of Ka'b ibn Malik, and the famous Arab poet, Hasan ibn Thabit, used to recite poetry for her.

Other than her tremendous intellectuality and sagacity, she was intensely pious and a devout worshipper.

How A'ishah Strengthened the New Roles of Women

Sayyidatuna A'ishah contributed significantly through her illustrious examples that set a new tone in academic, social, judicial and gender relations.

1. **She excelled intellectually.**

   Her tremendous intellectual growth and sagacity could only have developed in a spatial environment in which such growth was encouraged. Within the Prophetic household she must have been provided with the time and space to study, and she could not have been alone in this.

2. **She excelled academically.**

   She was renowned as a teacher. She had about two hundred students, of both genders, of whom some studied under her for long periods of time. These included 'Urwa ibn Zubayr, Qasim ibn Muhammad, Abu Salama ibn Abd al-Rahman, Masruq, 'Amrah, Safiyyah bint Shayba, A'ishah bint Talha, and Mu'awa 'Adwiya. (Siddiqi, 1982, p. 38) The fact that she was consulted by the Companions on matters religious, and also wrote on various disciplines within the religion of Islam, meant that her impact as a scholar, consultant and teacher must have been phenomenal if one considers that the new social order was still very young, and that many of the old attitudes towards women could not all have been wiped out by that time.

3. **She established religious precedents.**

   She laid the basis of an important principle of coordination between the Quran and the Sunnah. Her principle was later followed by Imam Abu Hanifa and Imam Bukhari. Even today, jurists solve problems in the light of her dictum of harmony between the Quran and the Sunnah.

4. **She participated on the battlefield.**

   Her involvement in the Battle of Uhud, albeit as a supplier of water to the wounded, reflected the new status acquired by women. It is reported by Anas, "I saw A'ishah and Umm Sulaym carrying bags. They filled them with water and gave it to the wounded to quench their thirst." ...Her participation in the Battle of the Camel in a leadership position further strengthened this new status, although she came off second best in the battle.

This battle occurred after the assassination of Sayyiduna 'Uthman (r), when, together with Talha (r) and al-Zubayr (r), she took up arms against Sayyiduna `Ali (r) demanding that the murderers pay the penalty for the crime. The battle took place near Basra. Sayyidatuna A'ishah (r) watched from a palanquin on the back of a camel and for this reason it was called the Battle of the Camel. Sayyiduna `Ali (r) was victorious. (Holt et al, 1970, vol. 1a, pp. 69-70)

5. **Her actions prompted divine revelation.**

She was part of events that "gave rise to" two rulings in the Quran. It is related by Dhakwan (r) that `Abdullah ibn Abbas told her during her final sickbed, "You dropped your necklace on the night of al-Abwa (after the Battle of Mutaliq, fifth year of the Hijrah) and the Messenger of God began to look for it until morning still found him in the campsite. The people had no water and so God revealed that they should do tayammum with good soil. (*This was the first ruling.*) What God allowed this community of lenience was through you. God sent down your innocence from above the seven heavens." (Ibn Sa'd, 1995, p. 53). This occurred when she was accused of infidelity by a faction hostile to her, and God declared her innocence in the Quran. At the same time God declared the necessity of four witnesses in such accusations. (*This was the second ruling.*) (Hodgson, 1977, p. 183)

6. **She achieved a high spiritual level.**

Her final words to `Abdullah ibn Abbas in this report were: "By the One who has my soul in His Hand, I wish that I had been something discarded and forgotten." This intense desire, during the last few hours of her life, to be "nothing", to want to approach her Lord "discarded and forgotten", to put all her achievements behind her; all these reflect a spiritual resignation of the highest level. She was destined to be with her husband (s) in the Hereafter. Her spiritual resignation reflected her imminent status. Aside from all her other achievements, her spiritual status "to be with her husband" stands as a peak of attainment that can be reached or nearly reached by all those who strive in that direction. Perhaps her words are also a lament for past transgressions.

Hafsa bint `Umar ibn al-Khattab

Sayyidatuna Hafsa was the daughter of Sayyiduna `Umar ibn al-Khattab who became the second Khalifah of Islam. Her mother was Zaynab, the sister of the Companion, `Uthman ibn Maz'un (radhiAllahu anhum). Hafsa had previously been married to Khanays ibn Hudhaifa (r), who died of wounds received during the Battle of Badr. She became the wife of the Messenger of God (s) when he expressed desire to marry her after her husband's death. (Siddiqi, 1982, pp. 40-41)

Hafsa's Distinct Qualities and Achievements

From among women and among Ummat al-Mumineen, Sayyidatuna Hafsa is renowned for the following qualities and achievements:

1. **She memorized the Quran.**
   She was one of the first *hafizahs* of the Quran. (Bashier, 1990, p. 47)
2. **She was devoutly religious.**
   She was deeply religious, steadfast in prayer and fasting. She was made aware during her lifetime of the Divine recognition of her piety and her status in the Jannah. However, because of her excessive jealousy, the Messenger of God (s) divorced her. (Bashier, 1990, p. 145)

   It is related from Qays ibn Zayd that the Messenger of God (s) divorced Hafsa bint `Umar. Her uncles, `Uthman and Quddama, sons of Maz'um, went to her and found her weeping. She said, "By God, the Prophet had not divorced (me) on account of being fed up with me." The Messenger of God (s) came and visited her and she put on her outer garment. The Messenger of God (s) said: "Jibril came to me and told me, 'Take Hafsa back. She fasts, and prays at night. She is your wife in the Garden.'" *(Ibn Sa'd, 1995, p. 58)*

3. **The Quran was placed in her care.**

   She played a vital role in looking after "the stock of holy scrolls and relics on which the Quran was inscribed during the lifetime of the Messenger of God (s) ... Her care and safekeeping of the Quran verses committed to writing were an integral part of the Divine promise to preserve the Quran as the perfect Scripture." (Bashier, 1990, pp. 144 &160)

   After the final editing of the Quran by Sayyiduna 'Uthman, this was also placed in her care and it became the standard copy of the Holy Script. An inestimable honor, the fact that this copy was given to her for safekeeping tells a large story of the particular status reached by women during and after the time of the Messenger of God (s).

4. **She engaged the Prophet (s) in religious and philosophical discussions.**

   "Before Islam, women were not allowed to hold opinions of their own or to object to anything their lords or masters chose to say. Islam decrees that a woman is an individual who has the right to think for herself and to express her beliefs as men do. She is a free, responsible being before God." (Al-Ismail, 1988, p.198) This newly acquired right encouraged Sayyidatuna Hafsa (r) to have long discussions with her husband on religious matters, discussions in which she strongly presented her views. Although her father Sayyiduna 'Umar (r) became concerned about the matter, her actions were an indication of the liberties women were allowed to enjoy in the new social dispensation.

Umm Salama (Hind) bint Abu Umayya Suhayl

Sayyidatuna Umm Salama (r) was the daughter of Abu Umayya Suhayl of the Makhzum tribe of Quraysh. Her mother was 'Atiqa bint Amir of the Bani Faras. She was originally married to her cousin, Abu Salama, a foster brother of the Messenger of God (s), who died of injuries he sustained during the Battle of Uhud. She was married to the Messenger of God (s) during the fourth year of the Hijra.

She was one of the first women who migrated to Madinah. She had originally wanted to migrate with her husband, Abu Salama, to that city but her tribe resisted. Her husband then left without her. To prevent her from leaving, the members of her tribe snatched her child, Salama, from her. Every day she would go out to Abtah in distress, crying bitterly. One day a relative of hers saw her condition. He said to her people, "Why do you torture her? Let her go with her child." They gave her permission to leave, and with her child she left for Madinah on a camel. She was on her own, traveling through the desert.

In Tu'nim, 'Uthman ibn Talha (then possessor of the keys of the Ka'ba) saw her and asked, "Where are you going?" She replied, "To Madinah." He asked again, "Is any one with you?" She replied, "God and this child are with me." 'Uthman decided to help her, and taking hold of the reins of the camel set out for Madinah. Sometimes, when she was riding the camel, he would walk at some distance behind her. When they reached Qu'ba, he said to her, "Now you may proceed to your husband who is staying here." 'Uthman returned to Mecca.

Commenting on 'Uthman, Umm Salama (r) said, "I have never seen such a noble man." The people did not believe her when she told them who she was. It was only later when some of the people went on Hajj, and she conveyed a message to her parents, that they realized that she was the daughter of the famous Abu Umayya. (Siddiqi, 1982, pp. 48-49)

Two Distinctive Contributions of Umm Salama

There are a number of events through which her involvement indicated a particular response to women's status as granted by Islam.

1. **She made an important public announcement.**
    During the siege of Banu Qurayza during the fifth year of the Hijra, Abu Lubaba was sent to the Jews to negotiate. He hinted to them that they might be killed. Since this information was confidential, he felt so much remorse that he had himself tied to a pillar in Masjid al-Nabawi, pleading for repentance.

When his repentance was granted, the Messenger of God (s) was staying with Sayyidatuna Umm Salama (r). He informed her that the plea of Abu Lubaba had been accepted. She was granted permission by the Messenger of God (s) to make the announcement about the acceptance of the repentance. She went to stand at the door of her apartment and called out in a loud voice: "Abu Lubaba, congratulations! Your prayer for forgiveness has been granted." (Siddiqi, 1982, p. 53) For a woman to make such an important announcement was unheard of prior to the coming of Islam.

2. **She advised the Prophet of God (s) on a crucial matter.**

She was with the Messenger of God (s) at the time of the Treaty of Hudaybiyah. When the treaty had been signed, the Messenger of God (s) instructed the Muslims to slaughter animals and shave their heads in order to exit the state of ihram.

The people were so disappointed with the terms of the treaty that they refused to comply. Thrice he ordered and each time they refused. The Messenger of God (s) went to his tent and complained to her. She said, "Do not say anything to anybody but you go outside, slaughter an animal and shave your head, to be released from ihram."

The Messenger of God (s) took her advice, and did as she suggested. When the people saw what he had done, they all came hurrying to slaughter their animals and have their heads shaven. Commenting on this, Imam al-Haramayn said, "The example of such a timely and accurate advice is not found (anywhere) in the annals of the history of women." (Siddiqi, 1982, p. 54) Of course, her suggestion reflected a penetrating understanding of human nature.

Intellectual Merits of Umm Salama

Sayyidatuna Umm Salama is well known for her sagacious intellect. Here we offer a few examples.

1. **She was a transmitter of Prophetic traditions.**

   Mahmad ibn Lubayd stated, "The wives of the Holy Prophet (s) were the treasure house of traditions, but A'ishah and Umm Salama (r) had no parallel." She transmitted 378 traditions (hadith), and countless Muslims acquired knowledge of ahadith from her.

2. **She learned recitation of Quran from the Messenger of God.**

   She acknowledged, along with Sayyidatuna A'ishah (r), "The Holy Prophet (s) recited each verse clearly and distinctly. He then taught us to recite." (Siddiqi, 1982, p. 58-59) She recited the Quran in the same style as the Prophet (s).

3. **She was a recognized authority on Islamic Jurisprudence.**

   She overruled the practice of `Abdullah ibn Zubayr on the praying of two cycles after the 'Asr prayer as he had been previously advised by Sayyidatuna A'ishah (r). Umm Salama said: "May God forgive A'ishah. She has misunderstood the matter. Had I not told her that the Messenger of God prohibited her to offer it?"

   Umm Salama and Sayyidatuna A'ishah overruled the verdict of Sayyiduna Abu Hurayrah (r) that the obligatory bath of *Janaba* should be performed immediately in the morning, otherwise the fast is broken. They indicated that the Messenger of God (s) fasted in a state of *Janaba*. (Siddiqi, 1982, pp. 60-61)

These notable qualities were strengthened by Umm Salama's deep-rooted piety, generosity and religious obedience. From her examples we learn that the women of her time, indeed those who carried the torch of Islam, were encouraged to develop their individual personalities and express their unique views with confidence.

Sayyidatuna Fatimah al-Zahra (r)

Sayyidatuna Fatimah (r) was the youngest daughter of the Messenger of God (s) from Sayyidatuna Khadijah (r), chronologically preceded by her sisters Zaynab, Ruqayyah, and Umm Kulthum (r), all of whom are included among the women pioneers of Islam.

One day she inquired of the Holy Prophet why she was called Fatimah. He said that it was so, because fire would not touch her soul. She was also called "Batool", because she devoted herself all out to God and fervently followed the dictates of the Prophet (s).

Fatimah resembled the Prophet (s) in countenance, gait, eloquence, bravery, and in general demeanor. Whenever Fatimah paid a visit to her father (s), it was his custom to kiss her on the forehead and make her sit in his seat.

He (s) often said, "Fatimah is part of me, and whoever angers her angers me, and whoever injures her injures me." It was customary for the Prophet (s) when departing on a journey the last person from whom he took leave was Fatimah, and when he returned she was the first person he saw.

Her courage was demonstrated on several occasions. Once in the mosque, when the unbelievers of Mecca had placed a camel's entrails on the back of the Prophet (s) when he was in the midst of reciting his prayers and in the position of sajdah, Fatimah ran to her father's aid and flung the offensive matter from his person and shouted at Abu Jahl and his associates.

She also participated in battles against the unbelievers and nursed her father's wounds. Throughout times of extreme poverty and hardship, she was known for her steadfast patience and service to others.

Sayyidatuna Fatimah (r) stands unparalleled in Islamic history as an individual of high spiritual caliber. She was extremely fortunate to possess the close proximity of her noble father, the Messenger of God (s), and later Sayyiduna `Ali (r) as her husband. Her unique position afforded her close contact with most of the leading Companions of both genders.

Thus, she lived in an environment dominated by the most advanced spirituality of all time, and it was her spiritual receptiveness within this environment that made her one of the most pious women of all time.

According to a Prophetic tradition (quoted by Siddiqi, 1982, p. 102): Among all the women of the world, Maryam, Khadijah, Fatimah and Asiya are sufficient to emulate.

Fatimah az-Zahra was married to Sayyidatun `Ali (r), the first cousin of the Prophet (s), for nine years. She died in her late twenties, leaving `Ali and their sons Hasan and Husayn (r), the beloved grandsons of the Prophet (s), each of whom grew to become highly honored figures in Islam. A third son, Muhsin (r), died in infancy.

The Prophet's Special Care of Fatimah

The guiding hand of her father (s) helped Sayyidatuna Fatimah (r) navigate challenges and prepared her for spiritual greatness. We quote some examples here:

1. **The Prophet (s) comforted her in their shared bereavement.** …(the death) of his daughter Ruqayyah … was the first bereavement they had suffered within their closest family circle since the death of Khadijah, and Fatimah was greatly distressed by the loss of her sister. The tears poured from her eyes as she sat beside her father at the edge of the grave, and he comforted her and sought to dry her tears with the corner of his cloak. (Lings, 1983, p. 161)
2. **The Prophet (s) joined her in marriage to Sayyiduna `Ali (r).** To his family he had already spoken of `Ali as the most fitting husband for her, but there had been no formal contract …It was only in the weeks which followed his return from Badr that he became certain that the time had come and he then spoke words of encouragement to `Ali in the wish that he should formally ask for her hand. `Ali was at first hesitant (but later) allowed himself to be persuaded. (Lings, 1983, p. 161)
3. **The Prophet (s) blessed her marriage.** (After the last guest had left the wedding celebration), the Messenger of God came and stood at the door and gave the greeting …He called for water and it was brought in a vessel and he washed his hands in

it (and in another narration: he rinsed his mouth in it). He called `Ali who sat in front of him, and he sprinkled some of that water on his chest and between his shoulders. Then he called Fatimah …and then he sprinkled some of that water on her. (Ibn Sa'd, 1995, pp. 16-17)

4. **The Prophet (s) invited her to spiritual excellence in the face of challenge.**

The couple lived in extreme poverty, and they performed menial tasks in the community to provide some income. One day her husband suggested to her that she ask her father for a servant from amongst the captives the Muslims had. Her father's reply to their request was, "I will not give you and let the People of the Bench be tormented with hunger. I have not enough for their keep; but I will spend on them what may come from the selling of the captives." (Lings, 1983, p. 168)

The People of the Bench, *Ahl al-Suffah*, were a group of emigrants who, because of poverty, were allowed to occupy the covered part of the mosque at night. They were fed from the rations of the wealthy. (Haykal, 1976, p. 178)

That night the Messenger of God (s) visited them, and said, "Shall I not tell you of something better than that which you asked for?" When they said yes, he said, "Words which Gabriel taught me, that ye should say *Subhanallah* ten times after prayer, and ten times *Alhamdulillah* and ten times *Allahu Akbar*. And that when ye go to bed, ye should say them thirty-three times each." (Lings, 1983, p. 168)

5. **The Prophet (s) Facilitated Her Reconciliation with `Ali.**

Habib ibn Abi Thabit said, "Some words passed between `Ali and Fatimah. The Messenger of God entered and `Ali made him a bed and he lay down on it. Fatimah came and lay down beside him. `Ali came and lay down on the other side. The Messenger of God took `Ali's hand and placed it on his navel and took Fatimah 's hand and placed it on his navel and continued until he had made peace between them." *(Ibn Sa'd, 1995, p. 18)*

6. **The Prophet (s) declared, "Fatimah is a limb of my body."**
When Sayyiduna `Ali (r) sent a message to the daughter of Abu Jahl for marriage, the Messenger of God (s) ascended the pulpit and said:

> *Indeed Bani Hashim want to marry their daughter with `Ali ibn Abi Talib and seek permission from me. But I won't give them permission; I would never give them permission. Of course, Ibn Abi Talib can do so after divorcing my daughter. Fatimah is a limb of my body. Anyone who offends her would offend me. Indeed Fatimah is a part of me, and I fear that (by her husband taking another wife) she may be put to trial in regard to her religion …I do not make unlawful what is lawful nor do I make lawful what is unlawful. By God! The daughter of the Messenger of God and the daughter of the enemy of God cannot gather together.* (Siddiqi, 1982, p. 102)

As a result of this, Sayyiduna `Ali (r) did not marry a second time during the lifetime of Sayyidatuna Fatimah (r).

7. **The Prophet (s) said, "You will be the swiftest of my family to join me."**
A'ishah said, "I was sitting with the Messenger of God (s) when Fatimah came walking with the same gait as the Messenger of God. He said, 'Welcome, my daughter.' He had her sit at his right or his left and whispered something to her and she wept. Then he whispered something to her and she laughed. I said. 'Why did I see you laugh so soon after weeping? The Messenger of God singled you out for something and then you wept. What did the Messenger of God whisper to you?' She said, 'I will not divulge his secret.' "When the Messenger of God (s) died, I asked her again and she said, 'He said: Jibril used to meet me every year and repeat the Quran to me once. This year he has come to me twice and repeated it to me. I think that my end is near. I am the best precursor for you. He added: You will be the swiftest of my family to join me. I wept at that. Then he said: Are you not content to be the mistress of the women of this community, or the women of the worlds?' She said, 'I laughed at that.'" (Ibn Sa'd, 1995, pp. 18-19)

Salma said, "Fatimah, the daughter of the Messenger of God, was ill while we were with her. On the day she died, `Ali had gone out. She said to me, 'Pour a bath for me.' So I poured a bath for her and she washed in the best manner in which she used to wash. Then she said, 'Bring me my new clothes.' So I brought them to her and she put them on. Then she said, 'Put my bed in the middle of the house.' I did that and she lay down on it and faced qibla. Then she said to me, 'Mother, I will die now. I have washed, so do not let anyone uncover my shoulder.' She said, "She died. Then `Ali came and I told him. He said, 'By God, no one will uncover her shoulder.' He took her and buried her with that ghusl."

Ahli Bayt - People of the House

Sayyidatuna Fatimah 's (r) position in Islam has to be considered in relation to the love and respect for the Messenger of God (s), her devotion to him, to his family and descendants, and the Mothers of the Believers.

God Almighty said:

> *God wants to remove impurity from you, People of the House. (33: 33)*

The phrase "People of the House" is explained in a number of traditions:

> *Zayd ibn Arqam related that the Messenger of God said, "I implore you by God! The People of my House!" three times. We asked Zayd who constituted the People of his House, and he said, "The family of `Ali, the family of Ja'far, the family of 'Uqayl, and the family of al-`Abbas."*

> *The Prophet said, "I am leaving you something, taking hold of which will prevent you from going astray: the Book of God and my family, the People of my House. So take care how you follow me regarding them."*

> *`Umar ibn Abi Salama said, "God wants to remove impurity from you, People of the House," was revealed in Umm Salama's house. The Prophet summoned Fatimah, Hasan and Husayn and enfolded them in a garment and `Ali was behind him. Then he said, "O God! These are*

the People of my House, so remove all impurity from them and purify them completely!"

Sa'd ibn Abi Waqqas said that when the verse of mutual cursing (3:61) was revealed, the Prophet called `Ali, Hasan, Husayn and Fatimah, and said, "O God! These are my family." (Quoted by Qadi 'Iyad, 1991, p. 241-242)

Fatimah az-Zahra's Position in Islam

Various honors associated with Sayyidatuna Fatimah (r) reflect her unique standing in Islam. We list some here:

1. Her position as a member of the Prophetic household; also as a child of the Prophet (s) and Khadijah (r).
2. She received special mention and status in both the Quran and Hadith.
3. She is regarded as one of the four perfect women of all times, the other three women being: Asiyah the wife of the Pharaoh of Egypt and foster-mother of Moses; Mary, the mother of Jesus Christ; and, Khadijah, the first wife of the Prophet of Islam, and Fatimah's mother.
4. She was the only of the Prophet's (s) children to generate his progeny.
5. The special privilege of being personally nurtured by her father (s) for spiritual greatness, up to the time of his death.

Sayyidatuna Fatimah (r) is revered today by both men and women as one who, through self-effacement, attained the highest spiritual level. Although in a sense she had many advantages, she responded to life's extreme challenges in a way that brought her close to her Lord, and continues to serve as a shining example for us all. Her accomplishment demonstrates the vast overflow of Divine blessings for those who seek their Lord. And God knows best!

Glossary of Terms

Abu – father.

Abu Bakr – the closest companion of the Prophet and first man to embrace Islam; father of A'ishah, wife of the Prophet; migrated from Mecca to Madinah with the Prophet; first appointed successor of the Prophet; known as the most generous of the Companions.

Abu Talib – uncle of the Prophet; father of `Ali.

Abdul Muttalib – the Prophet's paternal grandfather and an influential leader of the Quraysh tribe. Became the Prophet's guardian when his mother died.

Adab – etiquette; manners; propriety. Islamic teachings emphasize the application of adab to all actions. It has been said, "To know adab is to know Islam."

Ahl as-Sunnah, wal Jama`ah – People of the Sunnah, and Majority.

Ahlul Bayt – People of the House, a term reserved for the Prophet's family.

Ahlul Kitab – People of the Book, a reference to followers of the Torah (Old Testament) and the Injeel (New Testament), the divine books revealed to Prophets Moses and Jesus, respectively.

Akhira – the Afterlife.

al – the

al-Amin – the Trustworthy; a name attributed to the Prophet.

Alayhim as-salam – "And upon them be peace", spoken upon mention of prophets and messengers; abbreviations include A.S., a.s. and (a).

Allah – The One True God, Who is independent of and Creator of all things, Who has no mother, son, or partner; The Supreme Deity and Universal God for all people, times and places, Who sent down a consistent message through His Prophets and Messengers, that humanity may be rightly guided.

Allahu Akbar – Allah is the Greatest.

Allahu Ahad – Allah is One.

`Ali, bin Abu Talib – first cousin of the Prophet and the first boy to embrace Islam; son of Abu Talib; husband of Fatimah, the Prophet's daughter; father of Hasan and Husayn; the fourth successor of the Prophet.

`Alim – scholar of Islam.

Alhamdulillah – *all Praise is due to Allah*; similar to "Praise the Lord"; hallelujah; alleluia.

Amir – leader.

Ansar – Helpers, Supporters; an honored title given to the people of Madinah, who swore allegiance to the Prophet and received him generously upon his migration from Mecca, helped establish the Muslim nation.

`Aqeeda – doctrine.

Ayah – a verse of Quran; plural, ayaah.

A'ishah – daughter of Abu Bakr; wife of the Prophet; a respected jurist, teacher and narrator of Prophetic Traditions; known for her exceptional memory, sagacity and acumen.

Adhan, azan – the prescribed call to prayer (in Arabic), pronounced five times daily. The one who calls adhan is known as "mu`azzin".

Bid`a – innovation; an act not attributed to the Prophet. Innovation in religion must be examined for its merit and on the basis of cause and effect. For example, the Prophet did not say his prayers while traveling on a bus, or recite verses of Quran across phone lines, or use a microphone to broadcast the call to prayer, each of which are modern-day innovations that make Islam more accessible and/or easier to practice.

Bismillah – In the Name of Allah; a serious phrase of seeking God's Help, commonly uttered by Muslims prefacing any given act.

Bismillah ar–Rahman ar–Rahim – *In the Name of Allah, the Most Beneficent, the Most Merciful*; a highly eminent phrase that precedes all chapters of the Quran; often prefaces correspondence, speeches, declarations.

Caliph – successor; "khalifah" generally refers to the supreme leader of the Muslim nation.

Din, deen – way, religion; Dee*n al–Islam,* the Islamic Faith.

Du`a – supplication; most often comprised of verses of Quran or hadith; normally recited after the prescribed prayers although encouraged at any time, by raising hands and uttering the supplication either in Arabic or other languages.

Eid, `Id – festivity; the two annual Eids in Islam; Eid al–Fitr, the celebration marking the end of Ramadan; Eid al–Adha, the celebration commemorating hajj, the pilgrimage to Mecca.

Fatwa – legal ruling by a qualified jurist; plural, fatawa.

Fatiha, al– – the opening; first chapter of the Quran.

Fatimah, az–Zahra – daughter of the Prophet; wife of `Ali; mother of Hasan and Husayn; acknowledged as one of the Perfect Women in Islam.

Fiqh – Islamic jurisprudence; faqih, a jurist; plural, fuqaha'.

Fisabilillah – *For the Sake of Allah,* a phrase connoting an action dedicated to the Almighty.

Four Imams, Four Caliphs – the four immediate successors of the Prophet to whom allegiance was obligatory throughout the Muslim world; namely, Abu Bakr as-Siddiq, `Omar ibn al-Khattab, `Uthman bin Affan, and `Ali ibn Abi Talib.

al–Furqan – the criterion; the Quran.

Ghusl – prescribed bath, requisite for prayer without which ablution is void; Must be performed after sexual relations, upon cessation of menstruation, forty days after childbirth, and before burial. Held as sunnah before many forms of worship, such as Friday congregational prayer, the Eid prayers, and performance of hajj.

Hadhrat – title of respect applied to Prophet Muhammad (s) as well as to other prophets and messengers, his family and companions, and great figures mentioned in Quran and Hadith; however the term is also used to address high persons who are present.

Hadith – authorized, recorded Prophetic Traditions on a host of topics, narrated by companions of the Prophet and transmitted down through time; plural, ahadith.

al-Hafiz – The Protector, an attribute of God; a hafiz of Quran has been tested by a board of scholars and certified as one who has memorized all of the Quran and can recite any verse or portion of it at random. Also a common Urdu salutation, "Khuda Hafiz" meaning "May God protect you."

Hajj – one of the five pillars of Islam; the pilgrimage at Mecca is incumbent on every Muslim in the world who has the financial means and the health to sustain the annual ritual at least once in their lifetime; male, hajji; female, hajjah; plural, hujjaj, hajeej.

Halal – lawful; permissible.

Haraam – unlawful; forbidden; prohibited.

Haram ash-Sharif – a term applied to three of the Muslim world's holiest sites, i.e. the Holy Ka`ba in Mecca; the Prophet's Mosque in Madinah; the al-Aqsa Mosque in Jerusalem.

Hasan – grandson of the Prophet; son of `Ali and Fatimah, who became a great leader and imam.

Husayn – grandson of the Prophet; son of `Ali and Fatimah, who also became a great leader and imam; martyred at Karbala in Iraq.

Hijra – migration; refers to the Islamic calendar which commences with the date when the Prophet migrated from Mecca to Madinah; (adj.) hijiri.

`Ibadat – worship.

Iftar – food or meal with which the fast is broken at sunset.

Ihsan – the state of divine proximity mentioned in the hadith, "To worship God as if you see Him…"

Ijma' – consensus of Muslim scholars.

Imam – one who leads the congregational prayer; also, an elite scholar; one responsible for the mosque, its leader.

Imam ash–Shafi`i – an eminent scholar and founder of one of the great schools of Islamic jurisprudence.

Insha'Allah –*If God Wills,* spoken at the time of making a commitment, with recognition that nothing is granted without God's permission.

Iqamah – a lesser version of the adhan, recited just before the prayer commences.

Islam – the way of submission to the Divine Will.

Jannah – Heaven; Paradise.

Jahannam – hell; hellfire.

Jihad – struggle; in a narrow sense, understood to mean "war" or military exercise or engagement. "Jihad al–Akbar, "the great struggle" refers to the highest level of self-discipline that brings one closest to the Almighty as a result of conquering one's ego.

Ka`ba – also "Bayt Allah", God's House; originally built in Mecca by Prophet Abraham and his son as a tribute to The One God; considered by Muslims as the center of the world; the direction Muslims face when offering prayer; the site of the annual Muslim pilgrimage, hajj.

Khadijah, al–Kubra – first wife of the Prophet and mother of his children; respected member of the Quraysh tribe; the first woman to embrace Islam; commonly acknowledged as one of the perfect women in Islam.

Khatam, al-Mursaleen – final; finish; end; finality of messengerhood.

Kufr – state of unbelief; kafir, one who does not believe in God.

La ilaha illallah – there is no God but the One True God.

Kalima tush-Shahadah – the Muslim Creed of Faith, namely, *Ash-hadu anla ilaha illallah, wa ash-hadu anna Muhammadan Abduhu wa Rasuluh* "I bear Witness that there is no God but God, and I bear Witness that Muhammad is the Servant and Messenger of God."

Madinah – the city to where the Prophet migrated from Mecca and established the Muslim nation; burial place of the Prophet; second holiest place in the Muslim world.

Madhhab – a legal method or school of Islamic law; generally refers to Hanafi, Shafi'i, Maliki, Hanbali and Jafari schools.

Maghrib – sunset; west; evening prayer of the five daily prayers, offered when the sun sets; "al-Maghrib", common Arab reference to Morocco.

Makkah, Mecca – location of the Ka`ba; birthplace of the Prophet; see *Qiblah*.

Masha'Allah –This is what God has chosen, determined or willed; attributes the source of all good to God.

Mi`raj, an Nabi – ascension; the heavenly ascension at divine invitation whereby the Prophet physically rode the heavenly transport Buraq from Mecca to Jerusalem, then ascended from this world through all the levels of Heaven. The occasion is broadly celebrated as a holy day throughout the world.

Muhammad bin `Abdallah – the Prophet; Muhammad son of Abdallah.

Mu'min – believer.

Mushrik – see *Shirk*.

Muslim – one who submits to God's Will; a follower of Islam; feminine, muslimah.

Nabi, nabi Allah – prophet; prophet of God; plural, anbiyya. Islam teaches that 124,000 prophets were sent to every nation and people as reinforcers of the Divine Message, that God is One and Muhammad is His Messenger. Some prophets were also messengers, such as Adam, Noah, Abraham, Moses, Jesus and Muhammad (s).

Nafs; an-nafs al-ammara – the lower self from which base desires emanate.

Qiblah – direction in which Muslims face to say their prayers, i.e. Mecca.

Qiblatain – "two qiblahs"; refers to Jerusalem, which was the first qiblah to which Muslims prayed, and Mecca, the city to which the qiblah was changed during the Prophet's lifetime.

Qira'at – recitation of Quran.

Qudsi Hadith – divine communication direct from God to the Prophet, which was other than a revealed verse of Quran.

Quran – Word of God Almighty; the divine book of Muslims revealed to the Prophet over 23 years, brought down by the Angel Gabriel; the core of Islamic law and comprehensive guidance which governs all aspects of life for Muslims.

Quran Majeed – the Glorious Quran.

Quraysh – an influential, pagan Arab tribe that held the reins of power at the advent of Islam; boycotted the Prophet and militarily opposed the Muslims.

Rabb, Rabbi – Lord; my Lord.

Rabbil `Alameen – Lord of all the Worlds; a phrase included in al–Fatiha, the Lord's Prayer of Muslims and opening chapter of the Quran.

Radhi Allahu anhu – God be well pleased with him; anhu connotes "him"; anha connotes "her"; anhum connotes "them".

Rak`at – one complete cycle of the prescribed Muslim prayer, which is comprised of either two, three or four cycles.

Ramadan – the month of fasting; the ninth month of the Muslim calendar; the month the first revelation of Quran was brought down; in which the Night of power occurs; one full reading of Quran during Ramadan is highly praised.

ar-Rasheed – the Rightly Guided; a name attributed to the Prophet.

Rasool, Rasool Allah – messenger, Messenger of God; refers to Prophet Muhammad. God sent many messengers to deliver His Message to people of all regions and eras. Some messengers were distinguished with a Code of Law, such as Abraham, David, Moses, and Muhammad (s).

Ruh – the soul; the spiritual self which separates from the physical self at the time death.

as-Siddiq – the Truthful, a name associated with many prophets as well as Muhammad (s); also a name of his dear companion, Abu Bakr.

Sahabah – Companions of the Prophet; those who saw or met the Prophet during his lifetime, or who were physically in his presence. The Sahabah narrated the greatest volume of Prophetic Traditions known as Hadith.

Sahur – pre-dawn food or meal specifically taken before the fast commences.

Sajdah – prostration, a prescribed component of prayer reserved exclusively for worship of God; also, sujud.

Salaf –reference to the Sahabah (Prophet's Companions), and the next few subsequent generations of Muslims.

Sallallahu alayhi was salam – May the Peace and Mercy of God be upon him; an expression applied exclusively to Prophet Muhammad. Abbreviated versions include p.b.u.h., s.a.w., s.a.w.s, and s.

Salat – prayer; also known as namaz (Urdu). The five compulsory daily prayers are known as Fajr (morning), Zuhur (midday), `Asr (afternoon), Maghrib (evening), and `Isha (night).

Sawm – fasting.

Sayyiduna – title of great respect applied to Prophet Muhammad (s) as well as to other prophets and messengers, his family and companions, and great figures mentioned in Quran and Hadith; also Syedna, Syedina, Sayyidina (masc.); Sayyidatuna, Syeda, Sayyida (fem.). When addressing one who is present with effective language connoting respect, the term Sayyid (masc.) and Sayyida (fem.) are also used.

Shaytan – Satan.

**Shi`a** – supporters of Ahlul Bayt; followers of the Ja`fari madhhab.

Shirk – associating partners with God; said to be the only sin God will not forgive; mushrik, one who associates partners with God.

Subhanahu wa ta`ala – Glorified and Exalted, in exclusive reference to God.

Sunnah – example of the Prophet, illuminated by his words and deeds.

Surah, surat – a chapter of Quran; Surat al-Fatiha, meaning "chapter of Fatiha".

Tabi`een – the third generation of the early Muslims, who lived after the passing of Prophet Muhammad.

Tasawwuf – the Islamic science that promotes human spirituality and helps one reach the state known as "ihsan".

Tasbih, tasabih, masbaha – rosary; prayer beads used to enumerate both prescribed and superogatory supplications.

Tazkiyyah, an-nafs – purification; the state of purifying and disciplining of the lower self, ego.

`Umar ibn al-Khattab – close companion of the Prophet; father of Hafsa, the Prophet's wife; second Caliph who advanced Islam beyond the Arabian Peninsula and defeated both the Roman and Persian Empires – two oppressive superpowers; liberated Jerusalem from Roman control; it is said Satan feared him.

**`Ulama** – plural of `alim; scholars.

Umm – mother; ummi, my mother; ummul, mother of.

Ummat al-Mumineen – Mothers of the Faithful, a title reserved exclusively for the wives of the Prophet.

Umra, umrah – the lesser hajj; includes all the rituals of hajj with the exception of the visit to `Arafat; pilgrimage performed at times other than days allocated for hajj.

Ummah – literally, "nation"; understood to mean the global body of Muslims.

Usool – principles; sciences; usool al-fiqh, principles of jurisprudence.

`Uthman – Companion of the Prophet and his third successor; original compiler of the Quran in book form; distinguished as "Thu-noorayn", one with to sources of light, for marrying two of the Prophet's daughters.

Wahi – divine revelation intended for chosen prophets and messengers, which was completed with the revelation to Prophet Muhammad (s) and will not occur again.

Wudu – prescribed ablution; a requisite of prayer, reading the Quran.

Bibliography

Al-Ismail, T. 1988. *The Life of Muhammad.* Jeddah: Abul-Qasim Publishing House

Ali, A.Y. undated. *The Holy Quran – Text, Translation and Commentary.* Beirut: Dar al-Arabiyyah

Al-Nawawi, A.Z.Y. undated. Riy*adh al-Salihin,* vol. i-ii (translated by S.M. Madni Abbasi). Beirut: Dar al-Arabia

Ansari, F.R. 1986. The Quranic Foundations and Structure of Muslim Society, vol. 1-2. *Karachi: Elite*

Aspects of Pre-Islamic Marriage, undated (www.witness-pioneer.org/vil/Books/SM_tsn/ch1s4.html)

Assad, M. 1980. *The Message of the Quran.* Gibraltar: Dar al-Andalus

Ayoub, M.M. 1992. *The Quran and its Interpreters,* vol. i-ii. New York: State University of New York Press

Badawi, J.A. undated. *The Status of Women in Islam*)

Bashier, Z. 1990. *Sunshine at Madinah.* Leicester: The Islamic Foundation

Doi, Abdur Rahman I. undated. *Women in the Quran and the Sunnah.*

Fisher, H.A.L. 1966. *A History of Europe.* London: Collins

Gibb, H.A.R. & Kramers, J.H. 1974. *Shorter Encyclopaedia of Islam.* Leiden: E.J. Brill

Haykal, M.H. 1976. *The Life of Muhammad.* American Trust Publications

Hell, J. 1943. *The Arab Civilization.* Lahore: Shaikh Muhammad Ashraf

Hodgson, M.G.S. 1977. *The Venture of Islam, vol. 1.* University of Chicago Press

Holt, P.M., Lambton, A.K.S. & Lewis, B. (eds) 1970. *The Cambridge History of Islam, vol. 1a.* Cambridge University Press

Hughes, T.P. undated. *Dictionary of Islam.* Lahore: Premier Book House

Ibn Sa'd, M. 1995.*The Women of Madinah.* London: Ta Ha Publishers

Iqbal, A. 1967. *The Culture of Islam.* Lahore: Institute of Islamic Culture

King, K. undated. *Women in Ancient Christianity: The New Discoveries* (www.pbs.org/wgbh/pages/frontline/shows/religion/first/women.html)

Khan, M.M. (trans.) undated. *Sahih al-Bukhari.* Madinah: Islamic University

Lings, M. 1983. *Muhammad.* India: Islamic Book Printers

Lone, A.E. undated. *The Position of Women in Pre-Islamic Arabia*

Najaar, A. 1992. *Selected Stories from the Quran*. Cape Town: Al-Khaleel
    Publications

The Status of Women in the Gospels (www.religioustolerance.org/cfe_bibl.htm)

Qadi 'Iyad, 1991. *Muhammad Messenger of Allah – Ash-Shifa*. Granada: Madinah
    Press

Siddiqi, M.S. 1982. *The Blessed Women of Islam*. Lahore: Kazi Publications

Soorma, C.A. 1929. *Islam's Attitude Towards Women and Orphans*.
    Woking: The Trust

Statements on the Status of Women by Christian Leaders and Commentators.
    (www.religioustolerance.org/life_bibl.htm)

General Index

Index of Verses from the Quran and Holy Traditions (Hadith)

Index of Prophets and
Blessed Women From Biblical Times

Index of Family Members, Companions and their Descendants (r)

Index of Places

Other Available Titles

In the Mystic Footsteps of Saints
Sufi Wisdom Series
By Shaykh Muhammad Nazim Adil al-Haqqani
Retail Price: $10.99

Narrated in a charming, old-world storytelling style, this highly spiritual series offers several volumes of practical guidance on how to establish serenity and peace in daily life, how to heal from emotional and spiritual scars, and discover the role we are each destined to play in the universal scheme. Written by Shaykh Nazim Adil al-Haqqani, a descendant of best-selling poet and Sufi mystic Jalaluddin Rumi. Paperback. Average length 175 pp.

Muhammad: The Messenger of Islam
By Hajjah Amina Adil
ISBN 1-930409-11-7
Retail Price: $21.99

Since the 7th century, the biography of Islam's Prophet Muhammad has shaped the perception of the religion and its place in world history. English biographies of Muhammad -- founder of the faith which currently claims 1.5 billion followers -- have characteristically presented him in the light of verifiable historical authenticity. MUHAMMAD: THE MESSENGER OF ISLAM goes one step further in skillfully etching the personal portrait of a man of incomparable moral and spiritual stature, as seen through the eyes of Muslims around the world. Compiled from classical Ottoman Turkish sources and translated into English, this comprehensive biography will be of interest to scholars of Islam and to all who seek to understand the essence of the faith, which is deeply rooted in the life example of its prophet. This esteemed biography not only details Muhammad's life, it also includes mystical secrets that Muslims believe were granted to the prophets who preceded him in the Holy Land and in other regions of the Middle East. This impressive biographical work deftly weaves quotes from authentic religious texts with ancient lore, resulting in a compelling, unforgettable read. Paperback. 608 pp.

www.ingramcontent.com/pod-product-compliance
Lightning Source LLC
Chambersburg PA
CBHW031131020426
42333CB00012B/324